Impossible Journey: The Story of the Victoria Land Traverse 1959–1960, Antarctica

by

John G. Weihaupt
Professor Emeritus
Department of Geology
University of Colorado Denver
Denver, Colorado 80217
USA

Alfred W. Stuart
Professor Emeritus
Department of Geography and Earth Sciences
University of North Carolina at Charlotte
9201 University City Blvd
Charlotte, North Carolina 28223-0001
USA

Frans G. Van der Hoeven
Department of Geophysics
Delft University of Technology
Postbus 5, 2600 AA Delft
The Netherlands

Claude Lorius
Laboratoire de Glaciologie et Géophysique de l'Environnement
54, rue Molière, BP 96
F-38402 Saint-Martin d'Hères cedex
France

William M. Smith
Professor Emeritus
University of Wisconsin–Green Bay
2420 Nicolet Drive
Green Bay, Wisconsin 54311
USA

THE
GEOLOGICAL
SOCIETY
OF AMERICA®

Special Paper 488

3300 Penrose Place, P.O. Box 9140 ▪ Boulder, Colorado 80301-9140, USA

2012

Published by The Geological Society of America, Inc.
3300 Penrose Place, P.O. Box 9140, Boulder, Colorado 80301-9140, USA
www.geosociety.org

Printed in U.S.A.

GSA Books Science Editors: Kent Condie and F. Edwin Harvey

Library of Congress Cataloging-in-Publication Data

Weihaupt, John G.
  Impossible journey : the story of the Victoria Land Traverse 1959–1960, Antarctica /
by John G. Weihaupt...[et.al.].
    p. cm. — (Special paper ; 488)
  Includes bibliographical references and index.
  ISBN 978-0-8137-2488-1 (pbk.)
  1. Victoria Land (Antarctica)—Discovery and exploration—American. 2. Victoria Land (Antarctica)—
Description and travel. 3. Victoria Land (Antarctica)—History—20th century. I. Title.

  G627.W42 2012
  919.89—dc23

                                                              2012006070

Cover: *Mosaic of Antarctica* (MOA) cloud-free image of Antarctica from the Moderate Resolution
Imaging Spectrometer onboard NASA's Terra and Aqua satellites, 2005. Courtesy of the National
Aeronautics and Space Administration.

10 9 8 7 6 5 4 3 2 1

Dedication

This book is dedicated to our predecessors—

Those Antarctic adventurers who went before.

Contents

Foreword

Impossible Journey

This remarkable book, *Impossible Journey: The Story of the Victoria Land Traverse 1959–1960, Antarctica,* provides an unvarnished account of Antarctic exploration and scientific data gathering during a four-month period, a half-century ago, in the remote, desolate, unusually harsh, and unexplored deep interior of Antarctica. From the era of the International Geophysical Year (IGY), we have thousands of Antarctic scientific papers, but we have few accounts of the history of the explorations as they truly occurred, and as they were associated with the scientific activities and discoveries made by the adventurers. Without such personal firsthand accounts, there can be no meaningful synthesis of science with the all-important history of science that accompanies it. The arrival of *Impossible Journey* fills this void.

Successful expeditions to Antarctica require remarkable comprehensive planning. Great attention must be given to specific times and places, to equipment, supplies, logistics, support—to the selection of participants—and to the purpose for going there! Once launched, each expedition takes on a unique character of its own, a consequence of these factors, and of the team that's been assembled. Few of us understand all of the subtleties of such expeditions—we weren't there! We rely instead on the accounts of those who were, to understand as best we can, the true nature of the undertaking. The *Impossible Journey* is the account of one such expedition.

The years 1955 to 1960 were witness to an international reawakening to the need for Antarctic exploration, and the science needed to comprehend the continent. What followed took place against a backdrop of Cold War politics, territorial claims, natural resource potential, and the need for international governance to protect this final Earth frontier. The IGY provided the rationale for an exploratory and scientific assault on the continent, with programs in the atmospheric, meteorological, oceanographic, geophysical, geological, and glaciological sciences. The contributions of these efforts would have far-reaching implications for our understanding of our planet and for global scientific theories and hypotheses that were evolving dramatically in that decade. Science planning and experience in this essentially unexplored region of the world were rudimentary, and remote areas would be visited for the first time. Reprints of maps and charts from the "Heroic Era" (1901–1914) were often the only guides to known or imagined regions, and then only of areas that extended little more than tens of miles inland from the coast. The effort would also train a generation of new young scientists, establish polar institutes, develop scientific rationales for the future management of our planet, and internationalize cooperative ventures among the participating nations. The formation of the Scientific Committee for Antarctic Research (SCAR) in 1958 was a prime catalyst of these endeavors, and the Victoria Land Traverse (VLT) would be a critical link in accomplishing these goals.

I once conjured up a vision of the perfect expedition, its wondrous experiences, and how the participants lived happily ever after. This of course is total fantasy! While one might become more efficient over time and learn to be better prepared for contingencies, we all recognize that the perfect expedition is an impossible undertaking. Antarctica is a very unforgiving place in which to gather scientific data. This is abundantly clear as we read *Impossible Journey*.

Remote field parties were normally quite small and populated by young men in their twenties. Most, though keenly interested in their science, volunteered out of a sense of adventure. Willing sacrificial lambs in a national and international scientific assault, most succeeded in earning their doctoral degrees after their adventure. Members of the Victoria Land Traverse team were no exception. It was an assemblage of young adventurers consisting first of eight and later seven mountaineer-scientists from four nations, the United States, New Zealand, France, and the Netherlands. If one had to identify two issues that hung over and overwhelmed this team, they would be the constant mechanical failure of the SnoCats and sleds, including the energy and ingenuity needed to keep them in operation, and the ever-present threat of crevasses. The role of "time" in remote field settings also was a challenge—the precise partitioning of time tends to evaporate, and one enters a strange time continuum without convenient markers by which to measure events. Days and weeks become merged, and only the position of the sun provides a clue. Work and sleep cycles are dictated by the vagaries of field operations. Fatigue and other complications appear as sleep and mealtimes drift around the 24-hour day. Over-snow traverses involve long stretches of travel over featureless terrain, and there is ample opportunity for one's mind to wander into seclusion, to engage in conversation with oneself, to indulge in visualizing imaginative and elaborate banquets, and to develop the well-known *"fifty-foot-stare-in-a-ten-foot-room."* One is rudely awakened from one's colorful and comforting trance, interrupted by a colleague loudly announcing the latest equipment failure, or by the discovery of a gaping crevasse! As our reading of *Impossible Journey* progresses, it becomes clear that operating quickly deteriorating equipment at high elevations, in frigid temperatures, on rough terrain eventually affected not only the condition of the equipment, but that of the team as well.

Comprehensive pre-season aerial photo surveys were not available for use on the traverse in the 1950s and 1960s. Black-and-white trimetragon photo coverage provided photos of some mountain topography, but the vast areas of relatively featureless inland ice plateau were poorly covered. Photo resolution was often poor, and crevasse fields were often indistinguishable from nearby safe areas. Crevasse fields were a constant concern and danger. The observant reader of *Impossible Journey* will follow not only the physical dangers and frustrations, but also the personal and interpersonal issues faced by the traverse team in the course of its long adventure. These things I know, for I trod the Dry Valleys of the continent and the far reaches of the Skelton Glacier in the era the VLT team was there.

Human behavior in remote and harsh environments is a fascinating subject. Candid comments offered here by traverse participants, on the innermost thoughts relating to themselves and their colleagues, are an important aspect of this account. Veterans of Antarctic fieldwork will be familiar with all that unfolds on the personal front in *Impossible Journey*. And there is much to be learned by anyone contemplating protracted isolation in the company of a few other human companions. Like me, Professor A.J.W. (Tony) Taylor has a long history of collaboration with the New Zealand Antarctic Research Program, particularly on matters related to expedition personnel selection and polar psychological issues. Taylor identifies many key issues about personnel selection and behavior. Here are two quotations from his book.

(Only) the most stable and experienced people … should be selected to work in Antarctica …, they are the least likely to become self-centred, dissatisfied, preoccupied, and inefficient … such (good) people are not … over-represented in society…. (Taylor, 1987, p. 95)

and

Seclusion is wasted on people of inferior character … waste it not… as wise men learn … that a little imperious hardship, a time of seclusion with only themselves to talk to, is most improving. For politicians and reformers it should be an obligation. (Frederick Greenwood, 1894, quoted in Taylor, 1987, p. xii)

Team members understood each other's strengths, frailties, and swings in emotion, and compensated for these day by day. They appear to have been well aware of their mental health, and consciously or unconsciously dealt with it quite comfortably. Despite abundant frustrations, they bonded. Each member of the party had his designated responsibilities, but, out of willingness and necessity, each developed secondary skills with amazing rapidity. In their words, "learn as you go, and pray you do it right." They became a closely knit and cohesive group, depending by necessity on one another. They were a "tribe." The book provides insight into this human psychology, young men doing their best against a battery of obstacles.

The Victoria Land Traverse 1959–1960 science plan focused on gravity and seismic geophysics, sub–ice sheet topography, glaciology, and topographic mapping. Their program complemented the work of other over-snow traverses on the Ross Ice Shelf, in Marie Byrd Land and from Ellsworth Station. Reconnaissance exploration in virgin territory is a mixed blessing. As illustrated in *Impossible Journey*, it is arduous, time consuming, and often unproductive, and plans are subject to constant change. Considerable time is often spent just documenting what's been traversed. However, serendipity is common. The team may be fortunate—it may stumble upon discovery. The Victoria Land Traverse 1959–1960 emerged with several major trophies as reward for the team's efforts. The discovery and delineation of the Wilkes Subglacial Basin and of the Wilkes Land Anomaly were particularly significant, and provided the impetus for detailed aerogeophysical surveys in later years. By comparison with present-day equipment and techniques, those available to the Victoria Land Traverse were primordial.

Preliminary results obtained by the Victoria Land Traverse 1959–1960 were published by geophysicist Jack Weihaupt in 1960 (*Arctic*, v. 13, no. 2) with more detailed accounts appearing in the team's subsequent science publications. A half-century has now elapsed since the completion of this traverse. What were the objectives of this geographic and scientific exploration? Who were the participants? How was the traverse accomplished? What were the challenges? How did it end? Where did their later careers lead them? Why, until now, was their story never told? *Impossible Journey,* coauthored by the original traverse participants, addresses these and many other questions. The polar community is now accorded an opportunity to experience, at firsthand, the rigors of life in the Antarctic trenches fifty years ago. We shall see that the International Geophysical Year posed more science questions than it answered. The merits of Alfred Wegener's continental drift hypothesis were still being debated within the international and Antarctic communities in 1960, and intellectual conversion from theories of crustal stabilism to mobilism was by no means complete. With the emergence of seafloor spreading and plate tectonic theory in 1962 and 1963, the significance of Antarctic geology in a global context assumed great relevance. The Victoria Land Traverse 1959–1960, occurring in this new phase of Antarctic exploration, was part of the thinking as the paradigm shift of plate tectonics came into general acceptance in the early 1960s. The hard-won, pioneer work of the Victoria Land Traverse contributed to and stimulated research associated with these new tectonic concepts.

Departure from the field and return to McMurdo Station and Scott Base after months of small group isolation is an abrupt and often traumatic experience. But you do get over it. The field party soon disperses to all corners of the globe. Some feel a sense of loss and loneliness with the realization that this unique group might never again convene. *Impossible Journey* leads us through this moment of truth and transition. Polar expeditions have a long tradition of reunions in later years, stimulated by the desire to recapture their "tribal" spirit from the past. The Victoria Land Traverse 1959–1960 participants held their reunions after many decades. They relived and analyzed the meaning of their venture, reaffirmed their bond as a team, and recalled specific days and events half a century later in amazing detail!

In earlier times, in the "Heroic Era" of Scott, Amundsen, Shackleton, and Mawson, official and personal accounts of expeditions appeared during or within a year or two of the expedition's conclusion, usually from the pen of the leader, senior associates, or highly esteemed prominent proponents of exploration and of science. International Geophysical Year and Trans-Antarctic Expedition accounts followed this publication model, and are usually absorbing, accurate, but often bland and sanitized accounts of activities and achievement. These accounts do not normally trespass into areas of extreme opinion, contentious issues, personality assessment, or the ugly nitty-gritty of daily expedition life. At a later time some members of these expeditions published more personal accounts, again avoiding contentious issues. Often decades elapsed before third-party biographers attempted subjective analysis and comparison of personalities, interpersonal relationships, and achievements. In the past decade or so, we have seen the appearance of a few books on Antarctic expeditions dating back half a century, books which are completely different literary beasts, and often written by the original participants much later, when they were in their seventies or eighties. *Impossible Journey* belongs to this last category and, without personal embellishment, falls between the works of the Heroic Era and the glossy high-tech Antarctic scene of today. Accounts are based on verifiable diary and report evidence, but are written with the benefit of five decades of hindsight, reflection, and career experience. These authors seem less restrained. They write with more emotion and conviction, and are unafraid to expose long-festering issues to the light of day. *Impossible Journey* is an honest rendition of—the way it really was!

We celebrate the contribution of this momentous historic and scientific endeavor. There are few other such contributions available to the public and to polar historians. Providing insights into the blood and guts of arduous exploration, it will be a valuable resource for historians and scientists alike. One hopes that scientists and explorers in the latter decades of the twenty-first century will gain inspiration from the Victoria Land Traverse 1959–1960's *Impossible Journey*.

Peter-Noel Webb
School of Earth Sciences
Ohio State University
Columbus, Ohio 43210

5 January 2012

Foreword

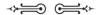

Both today's polar scientists and the general public might easily take for granted the pioneering work in Antarctica that built the foundation of our current understanding of the continent. *Impossible Journey* recounts the dramatic experiences of a major research effort undertaken over half a century ago, when snow vehicles regularly broke down and when the exact destination of a journey was not known at the outset. During the Antarctic summer of 1959–1960 the *Victoria Land Traverse* (VLT) measured the thickness of ice and the sub-ice topography in a remote, previously unexplored corner of the continent, and trialed snow analysis methods that contributed to our present-day understanding of global climate change. To obtain these data, the authors faced considerable personal risk and hardship, ranging from extremely low temperatures, whiteouts, enormous crevasses, repetitive equipment failures, long stretches of boredom, and, of course, challenging social dynamics that result from spending four months in isolation in a confined space with others. By comparison, today's polar activities are, thankfully, highly regulated and ensure a high degree of safety for researchers. The following firsthand account of the traverse reminds us that personal welfare was not always guaranteed in Antarctica, that meaningful polar research once required not weeks or months but years of personal sacrifice, and that the snows of remote Victoria Land preserve a chronology of weatherworn explorers as hard and unyielding as the ice they crossed. This is their story.

Placing the mode of transportation used by the VLT in the continuum of legendary polar explorations and modern research endeavors highlights the inverse relationship between the evolution of polar technology and the physical effort required for Antarctic work. On December 14, 1911, one hundred years before the publication of this book, Norwegian Roald Amundsen slid swiftly to the South Pole on the strength of dogs, often skiing beside the sleds and occasionally riding on the rails. He would later write, "I may say that this is the greatest factor—the way in which the expedition is equipped—the way in which every difficulty is foreseen, and precautions taken for meeting or avoiding it. Victory awaits him who has everything in order—luck, people call it. Defeat is certain for him who has neglected to take the necessary precautions in time; this is called bad luck" (*The South Pole,* 1912).

A scant hundred miles away, Englishman Robert Falcon Scott's polar party set out optimistically with a parade of ponies and a motorcar converted into Antarctica's first skimobile. Both methods of locomotion failed quickly and fatefully, and the party's southern progress reverted to the arduous task of man-hauling heavy sleds, called "sledging." They arrived at the pole on January 17, 1912, over one month after Amundsen. In the final days of his expedition, Scott wrote, "We took risks, we knew we took them; things have come out against us, and therefore we have no cause for complaint, but bow to the will of Providence, determined still to do our best to the last." Twentieth-century historians, who would scrupulously identify the shortcomings in Scott's plans and leadership, would nevertheless be moved when recounting the superfluous contents of his heavy sleds—thirty pounds of rock samples collected and transported to the end in the name of science. The bodies of Scott and his companions were found just eleven miles away from their next supply depot.

Scott's fellow Englishman and bitter rival Ernest Shackleton is remembered more for sailing 800 nautical miles across the ocean in a 23-foot-long life boat in order to save his crew than for being the first to reach the Polar Plateau in 1909. This epic boat journey followed his aborted attempt to traverse the continent in 1916. While his *Imperial Trans-Antarctic Expedition* failed, all of the men in his company survived, making

Shackleton a popular heroic figure, the subject of countless books and documentaries, and one of the most revered expedition leaders to this day.

The development of motorized equipment capable of surviving harsh polar conditions marked a new era of mechanized exploration in the early twentieth century. On November 28, 1929, American Richard Byrd led the flight of a Ford Trimotor, a three-engine transport airplane, from his base on the Ross Ice Shelf to the South Pole and back in just 18 hours and 41 minutes. The weight of the aircraft and four-man crew was initially too heavy to gain the altitude of the pole (9,306 feet) and they needed to dump empty fuel tanks and emergency supplies during the flight in order to complete the mission.

After a 44-year hiatus, men would again set foot on the pole on October 31, 1956, when George Dufek of the U.S. Navy landed there in a C-47 Skytrain aircraft. At that time, Byrd was commander of U.S. Navy *Operation Deep Freeze I,* which constructed U.S. bases at McMurdo Sound, the Bay of Whales, and the South Pole. Built during the Cold War, the Amundsen-Scott South Pole Station established a permanent U.S. presence at the pole before the Soviet Union had a chance to do the same.

In fulfillment of Shackleton's vision, New Zealander Edmund Hillary and Englishman Vivian Fuchs became the first overland parties since Scott to reach the South Pole in January 1958 as part of the *Commonwealth Trans-Antarctic Expedition* (CTAE). Fuchs used a team of three SnoCats, two Weasels, and one specially adapted Muskeg tractor to complete the first traverse of the continent, beginning near Vahsel Bay on the Weddell Sea and ending at Scott Base on the Ross Sea. On the opposite side of the continent, using three converted Massey Ferguson farm tractors from New Zealand and one Weasel, which was abandoned partway, Hillary began from Scott Base and laid supply depots for the second half of Fuchs' traverse between the pole and the Ross Sea, arriving at the pole fifteen days before Fuchs. Once Fuchs arrived, Hillary's party guided him down the Skelton Glacier and on to Scott Base.

Hillary's party accessed the Polar Plateau by navigating the crevasses of Skelton Glacier. Two years later, VLT members Jack Weihaupt, Al Stuart, and Frans Van der Hoeven would follow a similar route from Scott Base, over the Ross Ice Shelf, up the Skelton Glacier, to the Polar high plateau. Their experience with the Skelton as told in *Impossible Journey*, describes harrowing mishaps with yawning crevasses. Hillary describes similar challenges in his book, *View from the Summit*, with one notable exception: Hillary had extensive experience with negotiating enormous crevasses from his expeditions in New Zealand and the Himalaya, summiting Mount Everest with Tenzing Norgay just five years prior to the CTAE on May 29, 1953. By comparison, the members of the 1959–1960 VLT had little prior experience with crevasses; they learned as they went.

There were eight members of the VLT altogether, but the collective journal entries, notes, and memories of five researchers have provided the content of *Impossible Journey*. Team leader, Frans Van der Hoeven, was a Dutch seismologist with previous experience in the Arctic and the mining industry. Al Stuart, a glaciologist from Virginia, had prior experience working on the Greenland ice cap. Jack Weihaupt, a seismologist and geologist from Wisconsin, had previously led combat engineers in Korea and worked as an exploration geologist in the Andes. Claude Lorius, a glaciologist, had wintered at Charcot Station in East Antarctica the year before the VLT. Bill Smith, psychologist, VLT cook, and a member of the International Geophysical Year staff, asked to join the team to conduct a unique study: to research the researchers. Later, as a specialist in group dynamics at Walter Reed Army Institute of Research, the title of his 1966 *Psychological Reports* article would speak directly of the hardships endured by the expedition: "Observations over the Lifetime of a Small Isolated Group: Structure, Danger, Boredom and Vision."

For modern explorers, the SnoCats of the fifties and sixties have been replaced by a cleaner, greener variety of transportation that does not involve the direct burning of fossil fuels, wind power supplemented by classic sledging. On December 30, 1989, German Arved Fuchs (no relation to Vivian Fuchs) and Italian Reinhold Messner were the first to traverse Antarctica via the South Pole using only skis and sails held aloft in the wind. Several others have repeated this journey using similar means. One of the most inspirational expeditions was completed in February 2001 when Norwegian Liv Arnesen and American Ann Bancroft became the first women to traverse Antarctica as part of the longest known ski trek accomplished by women. Their achievement is of particular historical importance because the continent had long been "off limits" to female workers. Before 1956 when Russian marine geologist Marie Klenova became part of a Soviet oceanographic team that mapped part of the coast, the only women to visit the continent had been the wives of whaling captains and explorers. The U.S. National Science Foundation (NSF) refused female scientists permits to work in Antarctica until 1969, and the U.S. Navy refused to transport women to the continent for any reason prior to that time.

My own experience "on the ice" during the 2009–2010 field season involved far less drama and effort than past explorers and researchers. After being outfitted with cold-weather gear in Christchurch, New Zealand, I stepped into the bowels of a Boeing C-17 Globemaster military transport aircraft, plugged my ears, and strapped myself into a mesh cargo-netting seat for the five-and-a-half-hour flight to McMurdo Station. A single wooden sledge dangling from the wall above the ultra-modern pre-flight briefing room at the Christchurch airport was the only reminder of the century-old expeditions of Scott and Shackleton that departed *by boat* from Lyttelton Harbour, less than ten miles away. VLT members Al Stuart, Frans Van der Hoeven, and Jack Weihaupt also sailed from Lyttelton on December 14, 1958. Back then, the trip to McMurdo took thirteen days.

Once the plane was airborne, the flight crew gave us permission to peek through one of four tiny windows, each a hand's width in diameter, to the Earth's surface 45,000 feet below. For most of the journey there was nothing to see except tiny wave ridges etched on a vast ocean. Four hours into the trip the first part of the continent that came into view was the Transantarctic Mountains and the many glacial arteries that dissect their peaks. To our delight, the pilots invited a handful of eager, camera-toting neophytes into the cockpit to look down on this vast labyrinth of rock and ice that stretched to the horizon. Somewhere off the starboard side of the plane, beyond the last nunatak, was Victoria Land and the route of the 1959–1960 VLT.

Upon landing on the Ross Sea ice, we were transported the last miles in an all-terrain bus to McMurdo Station. Mount Erebus loomed 12,448 feet above the sea ice and greeted us with a wispy ash plume. Once we arrived, every critical aspect of our day-to-day lives—food, lodging, transportation, field gear—was organized and managed by Raytheon Polar Service, NSF's subcontractor for all things Antarctic. Devoted to Amundsen's code of exploration preparation, Raytheon rigorously trained each researcher in winter camping skills, basic first aid, radio use, and even helicopter seat-belt-buckle operation, before allowing them into the field. Most of the two-day training session took place on the Ross Sea ice several miles from McMurdo. To get there, we were transported inside a heated vehicle called a "Haglund," comfortably equipped with padded seats. By comparison, the SnoCats used by the VLT had only one seat for the driver and continuously leaked cold air onto the driver's feet. Our route to training camp wound past McMurdo's vast collection of antique polar vehicles—SnoCats, Weasels, Piston-Bullys, snowmobiles, cargo sleds—the workhorses of past expeditions now resting in a wide pasture of volcanic rock.

My own expedition to the field involved a thirty-minute ride from McMurdo to Lake Hoare Camp in the backseat of a Bell 212 helicopter. These machines are the modern beasts of burden for the Dry Valleys, and are frequently seen slinging a cluster of fuel barrels on the end of a 100-foot-long cable to a remote field camp. More often they are heard—their distinct "thwack, thwack, thwack" filling the valley air, breaking the Dry Valleys' silence. My helicopter flights in the Dry Valleys provided some of the most vivid memories and spectacular photographs of my month-long visit, and my research would have been impossible without their support. And yet, the inconsistency and variability of flight times caused the greatest amount of stress I felt during my entire experience.

For example, the day I departed McMurdo for the first time, my flight was moved *forward* four hours and I was given a 45-minute warning to "get my gear together." Later I would learn that *this* was modern Antarctic research—we were all at the mercy of the air support, the people who planned the flight schedules, and the moody weather which ultimately called the shots. After hearing me gripe, a seasoned polar veteran knowingly chuckled, "Welcome to Antarctica!"

Weeks later, I was trudging back to an isolated Quonset hut on the shore of Lake Fryxell while a storm was blowing in. Despite the 24 hours of sunlight, it was very dark and the mountain tops were covered in clouds. Rather than a sun-soaked glacial valley, I felt like I was walking beside an ice-covered New England lake at the beginning of a long winter evening. But I was not alone. Through the gathering snowflakes, I could see two Bell helicopters a quarter mile away, idling beside the hut with their rotors spinning. The weather was getting worse, and these would probably be the last flights of the day. I quickened my pace and wondered, "Do they see me? Are they waiting for me?" Miles up the valley at Lake Hoare Camp, a jovial group of researchers was gathered in a heated trailer to enjoy a freshly cooked meal, possibly some Scotch or a beer, and an evening of camaraderie. That was where I wanted to be—not here at this lonely outpost where I would be the only tenant. The thought made me walk faster, but to no avail. The tail of the lead helicopter rose slightly, the skids lifted a few feet off the ground, the body rotated and the bird gently lifted into the air. The second followed suit and the pair flew up the valley, over the Canada Glacier, and out of sight. A moment later, the last echoes of their blades reverberated off the distant valley walls. Their clap was replaced by the soft ticking of windblown snow against the hood of my parka, the only noise in a thick blanket of silence. I knew a helicopter would be back in the morning when the weather improved, but that gave me little solace. I grasped the door of the Quonset hut with my thickly gloved hand, pulled open the heavy barrier, and looked in at the dark, cold, empty tunnel that would be my shelter for the night. "Welcome to Antarctica," I thought.

For me, *Impossible Journey* is a reality check, reminding me of the relative ease of my greatest inconveniences. Others have experienced much greater trials than cutting short their work because of the early arrival of a helicopter, or loitering around for days on end because the weather is too bad to fly. In retrospect, even these hiccups were infrequent compared to the number of successful flights I made. We had internet access, DVD movies, and an ultra clear iridium phone with which I called my wife and family. Unlike the VLT crew, my radio always worked and I did not need to learn Morse code in order to communicate my needs. None of these amenities existed fifty years ago, when breakdown after breakdown caused the VLT to limp across Victoria Land. Most significantly, the modern polar researcher is shrouded in layers of protection—from clothing to training to constant oversight—which greatly reduce the likelihood of personal injury. I was never out of radio communication with either my colleagues or MAC OPS at McMurdo, and help, if needed, was never far away. But the VLT, like those before them, traveled through an unexplored landscape full of unmarked hazards. Their dramatic story of narrowly missing crevasses provides a vivid reminder of the great personal risk undertaken in the name of exploration and science. Today's multiweek research experience is highly sanitized by comparison.

Stories like *Impossible Journey* provide us with a firsthand account of polar history when the very idea of an annual Antarctic research program was in its infancy. These were the trail blazers. Their successes contributed to our knowledge of the coldest, highest continent on Earth, laid the foundation for future research, and demonstrated to politicians that this work was important and worthy of funding. Paramount to these achievements, this expedition into one of the last unexplored regions on Earth's surface must have inspired future dreamers, explorers, and knowledge-seekers. Did this leap across an ice sheet in 1959 help inspire the "giant leap for mankind" achieved a decade later? Did this view from the bottom of the world put into perspective the view of Earth from space? While the modes of transport have changed, the spirit of exploration, the thirst for knowledge, and the incredible personal strength have not.

Devin Castendyk
State University of New York, College at Oneonta

Preface

The U.S. Victoria Land Traverse (VLT) (Fig. P.1) took place from 1959 to 1960, more than half a century ago. Over the years some of us who were fortunate to have been selected for that journey have stayed in touch, have visited one another's homes, have met at professional conferences, or have gotten together whenever an opportunity presented itself.

In 1985, Jack Weihaupt arranged for members of the team to reunite at the Explorers' Club Annual Dinner at the Waldorf Astoria Hotel in New York City. A wonderful occasion, the VLT team was recognized from the podium for its "momentous scientific and historical journey" and for its contribution to polar exploration and research. In 2000, Jack arranged for the second official VLT reunion (Fig. P.2), again at the Explorers' Club Annual Dinner, at which the team shared remembrances of the joys and hardships of the four-month, 2,400-km expedition, the Victoria Land Traverse into the unexplored interior of northern Victoria Land in East Antarctica.

In June 2002, Jack arranged for the third reunion, inviting the VLT team to a gathering at his home in Evergreen, Colorado. In attendance were Frans Van der Hoeven, Lou Roberts, Al Stuart, Bill Smith, Jack Weihaupt (Fig. P.3), and Al Taylor (not pictured). Three of the team were unable to attend, namely, Claude Lorius, Arnie Heine, and Tom Baldwin. A great success, and enjoyed by everyone, over the period of three days the team reminisced about the traverse; shared slides and photographs; and shared published research papers, books, accounts of the journey, and maps of the region the VLT had traversed. We decided that the team should write an account, from logs and memories, of the Victoria Land Traverse, a book about the difficulties and the contributions of the undertaking. While memories had grown hazy, the VLT logbooks

Figure P.1. Back row: Frans Van der Hoeven, Claude Lorius, Arnie Heine, Bill Smith. Front row: Al Stuart, Lou Roberts, Jack Weihaupt, Tom Baldwin.

Figure P.2. Arnie, Bill, Al, Jack, and Frans at the second reunion at the Explorers' Club Annual Dinner at the Waldorf Astoria Hotel in 2000.

Figure P.3. The Victoria Land Traverse team reunion in 2002. (Left to right): Frans Van der Hoeven, Lou Roberts, Al Stuart, Bill Smith, and Jack Weihaupt.

and journals kept the effort on track. Jack, Al, and Bill supplied the photos, and Jack and Al provided the geophysical and glaciological accounts and data. Al and Jack provided maps, and Jack provided drawings of features and events for which there were no photographs.

The final product, *Impossible Journey: The Story of the Victoria Land Traverse 1959–1960, Antarctica,* is the result of the combined effort of Jack, Al, Frans, Claude, and Bill, and it represents the scientific, historical, and adventurous account of the Victoria Land Traverse, and of the nature and character of Antarctic exploration in that era.

> *I am a happy scientist, I work for IGY*
> *I measure this and measure that*
> *But no one tells me why.*

—Anonymous

Acknowledgments

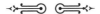

We wish to thank the other members of our Victoria Land Traverse team, Louis Roberts, Alfred Taylor, and Tom Baldwin, who also enabled the successful completion of the journey. We also wish to thank the U.S. Navy Squadron VX-6 for airdropping essential replacement spare parts for the vehicles and other needed survival supplies, and the U.S. Air Force for airdropping fuel drums without which the journey could not have been completed. We also want to express special thanks to Audrey Weihaupt, who edited and proofread the entire manuscript, and reviewed the copyediting and the page proofs. And to Audrey and Mary Louise Stuart we wish to express our appreciation for their patience, support, and endurance during the preparation, writing, and production of this book. We are also indebted to Dr. Peter Webb and Dr. Devin Castendyk for reading the manuscript and providing very helpful advice. Gratitude is expressed also to Patrick Jones, staff cartographer, Department of Geography and Earth Sciences, University of North Carolina at Charlotte for assistance in preparing cartographic materials, to Kurt Asplindh, photographer, for his assistance in preparation of selected photographic illustrations, and to Warren Harhay and David Holloway for computer-related assistance with the first draft of the manuscript. We want to express our special thanks also to Dan Howard, Dean, College of Liberal Arts and Sciences, University of Colorado Denver for financial support, and to April Leo, Managing Editor for GSA books, and the GSA staff for their impressive and expert management and production of this book. We want to recognize and thank the U.S. Geological Survey, the U.S. National Aeronautics and Space Administration, Landsat, and the British Antarctic Survey for providing the outstanding imagery of today's Antarctica. Finally, we wish to express our thanks to the U.S. National Science Foundation for financial support, and the University of Colorado Denver, the University of North Carolina at Charlotte, Delft University of Technology, the University of Wisconsin–Green Bay, and the Geophysical and Polar Research Center of the University of Wisconsin–Madison for administrative support.

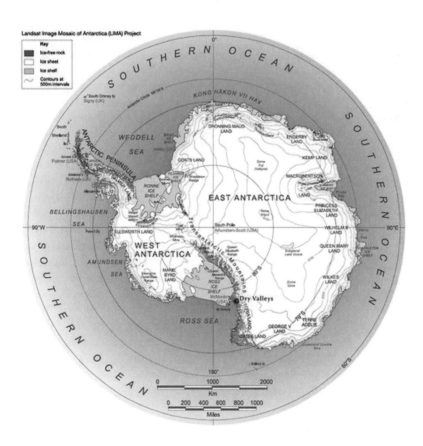

Map of Antarctica (with McMurdo Station and the Dry Valleys). From the U.S. Geological Survey Landsat Image Mosaic of Antarctica (LIMA) Project. (Courtesy U.S. Geological Survey.)

Introduction

No human endeavor is more fascinating than exploration, whether of Earth's oceans, its highest mountains, or the polar high plateau. There is a need, primeval as it surely is, to go where no one's gone before—to be the very first. The idea of an international research program to explore unexplored Antarctica is thought to have originated at a dinner party on April 5, 1950, in the home of James A. Van Allen, noted physicist for whom the "Van Allen radiation belt" is named. From the conversation at that gathering of English, Canadian, and American scientists, the idea emerged of organizing a major exploration of Antarctica. The effort would be in the tradition of the dim historic 1880s, and that of "The Heroic Age of Antarctic Exploration," of Captain Robert Falcon Scott, Captain Roald Amundsen, Sir Ernest Shackleton, and Sir Douglas Mawson. It would be based upon the model of international efforts in the 1930s. A proposal was then submitted to the International Council of Scientific Unions. Supported by some fourteen nations, the International Geophysical Year 1957–1958 (IGY) was the consequence of this initiative, along with the International Geophysical Cooperation (IGC) program that followed.

In anticipation of these efforts, the U.S. IGY effort in Antarctica was preceded by Operation Deepfreeze, which commenced in 1955 under the command of Admiral George Dufek. The operation provided for U.S. Navy Seabee construction crews to build and supply bases for the IGY research teams, including the McMurdo Naval Air Facility (NAF McMurdo), reflecting the role the U.S. Navy and Air Force would play in providing logistical support for the teams on the ground. This function was performed with remarkable effectiveness by these two military services, and the Naval Air Facility at McMurdo Sound would become the main point of entry into the continent, the jumping-off point for a host of research parties who would explore and survey the unknown interior.

The IGY evolved from this beginning to become an extraordinarily successful program of scientific research and international cooperation. Commencing in 1957, it eventually involved sixty-seven countries and 12,000 scientists at 2,500 stations ranging from the South Pole to ice islands in the Arctic Ocean. A key feature of the IGY was a common research agenda that would be followed by all participants, with the research data and findings to be housed in depositories around the world and made available to everyone. This was a remarkable achievement, coming as it did when tension between the United States and Western Europe, and the former Soviet Union was at its peak.

The central questions for the Antarctic component of the IGY concerned revealing the volume and structure of the continental ice sheet, the nature of the sub-ice topography, the influence of the ice sheet on global climate and global sea level, and the properties of Aurora Australis and the upper atmosphere, particularly the ionosphere. One of the most important parts of the program called for mounting geophysical traverses into the unexplored interior, traverses that would explore along a variety of routes over the continental ice sheet, gathering data on ice thickness, weather conditions, the annual accumulation of snow, and the nature of the land beneath the ice. The U.S. contribution to the IGY agenda in Antarctica was managed initially by the National Science Foundation, which later managed the successor U.S. Antarctic Research Program (USARP) following the official termination of the IGY in December 1958. USARP continued many of the IGY research programs in Antarctica.

While teams of marine biologists, atmospheric scientists, earth scientists, physicists, chemists, and solar system astronomers were assembled to work from permanent bases on the continent, USARP established the Oversnow Traverse Program to explore the unexplored interior of the continent. Initial oversnow traverses departed from several bases, such as Byrd Station in the interior of West Antarctica, Little America Station on the western edge of the Ross Ice Shelf, Ellsworth Station on the Filchner Ice Shelf, and Scott Base on Ross Island at the northern edge of the Ross Ice Shelf. A traverse led by Bert Crary departed Scott Base in 1958–1959. This traverse, entering the high plateau by way of the Skelton Glacier, explored the near eastern margin of the high plateau west of the Transantarctic Mountains, and was joined by Jack Weihaupt, Al Stuart, and Frans Van der Hoeven who would be tasked to explore the hinterland west of the Transantarctic Mountains the following year as the Victoria Land Traverse (VLT) team. While each of the USARP traverses covered large unexplored areas of the Antarctic continent, the VLT team was to conduct geophysical, geological, and glaciological research in the Victoria Land region of interior East Antarctica.

The VLT scientific-mountaineering team was composed of young adventurers, scientists with differing backgrounds and scientific specialties, and with diverse polar interests and skills. The VLT was later dubbed the "traverse of traverses" because of the duration and length of the VLT journey, and because of the severe challenges the traverse team met. These included extreme cold, long isolation, deprivation, physical hardship, endurance, monotony, unanticipated fields of hidden crevasses, potentially devastating equipment failures, catastrophic circumstances faced by the VLT team at the end of their journey, and the risk of abandonment of the team late in the season as the sun gave way to the six-month cloak of darkness. The book, then, is a daily account of the scientific, technical, and personal experiences of the members of the VLT team.

The Geological Society of America
Special Paper 488
2012

Impossible Journey

The Story of the Victoria Land Traverse 1959–1960, Antarctica

By John G. Weihaupt, Alfred W. Stuart, Frans G. Van der Hoeven,

Claude Lorius, and William M. Smith

Chapter 1

Planning and preparations for the Victoria Land Traverse

The Victoria Land Traverse (VLT) team of eight mountaineer-scientists and one mechanic, selected by the U.S. National Science Foundation (NSF) to undertake the journey, consisted of Frans Van der Hoeven, Jack Weihaupt, Al Stuart, Claude Lorius, Bill Smith, Arnie Heine, Lou Roberts, Al Taylor, and Tom Baldwin. Frans, a seismologist and leader of the VLT team, was from the Netherlands. Having worked in the mining industry in Turkey, Frans then worked with the United Nations after the Korean War in South Korea, where he was engaged in post-war reconstruction. Frans then spent five months in the Arctic during the International Geophysical Year (IGY), before wintering at New Zealand's Scott Base in Antarctica in preparation for the VLT. John G. (Jack) Weihaupt, also a seismologist, geologist, and mountaineer, was from the United States. From Wisconsin, Jack had explored the bush and barrens of Newfoundland for the Buchans Mining Company, subsidiary of the American Smelting and Refining Company; had commanded Combat Engineer troops with the Twenty-Fourth Infantry Division in Korea; and worked in the Atacama Desert and Andes Mountains for the Chile Exploration Company, subsidiary of the Anaconda Company, exploring for economic mineral deposits. With Frans, he would conduct seismic reflection and refraction investigations, measure variations in the Antarctic gravity field, and in the Antarctic magnetic field. Alfred (Al) W. Stuart, a glaciologist, was from the United States. From Virginia, Al, as a member of the U.S. Army, had worked with a research team that investigated frozen ground associated with the Greenland ice cap. Al would be responsible for glaciological research on the traverse, analyzing subsurface ice for temperature and density variations, in an attempt to uncover the historical behavior of Antarctic climate. Arnold J. (Arnie) Heine, an experienced mountaineer from New Zealand, also was a glaciologist. With Al, Arnie would dig glaciological pits in the surface of the East Antarctic continental ice sheet, and assist Al with temperature and density analyses of ice samples.

Claude Lorius was a glaciologist from France. As a specialist in isotope analysis of snow and ice, he had spent the winter prior to the VLT at France's Charcot Station on the coast of the Southern Ocean. Claude had also been a member of the French Adélie Land Traverse (ALT), which had established the end point (Apex Depot; ALT Station B-61; VLT Station 531) of the ALT. The VLT team would attempt to locate this end point in order to create a continuous seismic, gravity, and glaciological record from the Skelton Glacier to Charcot Station. Claude was to analyze the isotope contents of snow and ice from the ice pits dug by Al and Arnie, and from ice cores recovered by Frans and Jack. For his VLT isotope work, his discovery of the role of greenhouse gases in governing climate, and therefore the causes of global climatic change, Claude was eventually elected to membership in the French Academy of Sciences, a most distinguished honor.

William M. (Bill) Smith was from the United States. From California, Bill was a specialist in group dynamics and environmental behavior. Having served with the U.S. Army Air Corps in the South Pacific, Bill worked on the U.S. IGY staff, helped plan the U.S. Antarctic Research program, and during the previous summer (1958–1959) was the assistant IGY representative at NAF McMurdo. After the 1958–1959 season, he became a graduate student at George Washington University. Bill's task was to study the team's group structure and the environmental influences on the VLT team's behavior. Having requested that he be allowed to travel with the VLT team, the team agreed on the condition that Bill serve as cook. Louis J. (Lou) Roberts was from the United States. A topographic engineer with the U.S. Geological Survey, Lou was to be the navigator for the VLT, triangulating and taking daily sun shots to determine the traverse location, to enable location of the end point of the ALT, and to navigate the VLT team to the Transantarctic Mountains.

Alfred (Taylor) Taylor was from the United States. Also from Virginia, Taylor was a geologist with the U.S. Geological

Weihaupt, J.G., Stuart, A.W., Van der Hoeven, F.G., Lorius, C., and Smith, W.M., 2012, Impossible Journey: The Story of the Victoria Land Traverse 1959–1960, Antarctica: Geological Society of America Special Paper 488, 131 p., doi:10.1130/2012.2488. For permission to copy, contact editing@geosociety.org. © 2012 The Geological Society of America. All rights reserved.

Survey. Becoming ill shortly after the traverse left the head of the Skelton Glacier, Taylor was airlifted back to McMurdo, and then returned to the United States.

Thomas T. (Tommy) Baldwin, from the United States, was a U.S. Navy Seabee mechanic from Arkansas. Tommy had the daunting task of keeping VLT Tucker SnoCats running, and keeping the five-ton sleds functional. Without Tommy, it is unlikely that the VLT team could have remained in the field for the four months that were anticipated. Warren Jackman was a U.S. Navy photographer who would accompany the VLT team from Scott Base to the head of the Skelton Glacier and then be flown back to NAF McMurdo.

The Arctic Institute of North America (AINA) was contracted by the NSF to manage the staffing of the U.S. Antarctic Research Program (USARP). In the fall of 1958, AINA recruited Al, Frans, and Jack as the core of the VLT team. Prior to their departure for Antarctica, Jack visited the manufacturer of a rolling fuel transporter in Clintonville, Wisconsin, to evaluate the "Rolligon" for use on the traverse. The Rolligon consisted of two very large rubber tires mounted on a towing bar and was capable of transporting more than 400 gallons of fuel. In Davisville, Rhode Island, Jack also visited the U.S. Navy station, from which all cargo going to Antarctica was to be assembled and shipped, assisting in administrative duties, and in helping to manage the loading of supplies and equipment to be shipped to NAF McMurdo. At Davisville, with the help of Navy cargo specialists, Frans selected food stores for the traverse and marked, boxed, and readied them for shipment to NAF McMurdo.

Frans, Al, and Jack next visited NSF staff in Washington, D.C., regarding the policies of the NSF, and to make preliminary contact with staff with whom they were likely to communicate during the Antarctic effort. They also visited the Sperry-Piedmont Company in Virginia for familiarization with the company's crevasse detector, a potentially important piece of equipment. Next they visited facilities in San Antonio, Texas, for familiarization with the geophysical equipment to be used, conferring with the engineers at Texas Instruments Corporation, the company that manufactured the seismograph system to be used for seismic sounding of the sub-ice topography. After the visit with Texas Instruments, on November 21, 1958, the three men left for New Zealand on a Military Air Transport Service (MATS) flight from Andrews Air Force Base outside Washington, D.C. Joining them on that flight was John Russell, an Australian mechanic, who was slated to serve as mechanic on the traverse. After stops in Davisville, Omaha, San Francisco, Hawaii, Canton Island, and Fiji, the flight delivered them to Christchurch, New Zealand, on November 25, 1958.

Frans, Al, and Jack spent three weeks in New Zealand waiting for a ship to take them to "The Ice." In the interim, they toured the South Island, crossed the New Zealand Alps to the west slope, climbed the famous Franz Joseph Glacier (Fig. 1.1), and returned to Christchurch to consult with experienced polar scientists at the New Zealand Antarctic Program Office in Wellington. On December 14, 1958, Frans, Al, and Jack boarded the USS *Arneb*, a World War II troop transport ship at Port Lyttelton, departing in a small convoy led by the U.S. Coast Guard icebreaker, *Northwind*. Trailing these two ships was the USS *Nespelen*, a small tanker carrying a load of fuel oil to the U.S. base at NAF McMurdo, where it would anchor and provide fuel for the base for the winter.

Figure 1.1. Jack, Frans, and Al climb the Franz Josef Glacier in the New Zealand Alps, South Island.

Figure 1.2. Sir Raymond Priestley on the bridge of the USS *Arneb*, December 1958.

On board the USS *Arneb* was Sir Raymond Priestley (Fig. 1.2), who had served as a geologist on Sir Ernest Shackleton's 1907 Antarctic expedition, and again on Captain Robert Falcon Scott's 1910 expedition, which culminated in Scott's death and the deaths of his four companions on their return from their dash to the South Pole. This was Priestley's first visit to the Ross Sea area since 1913. Al, Jack, and Frans were quite moved as they stood with him on the ship's bridge, watching as Mount Erebus, the volcanic mountain on Ross Island, came into view.

The USS *Arneb* convoy reached NAF McMurdo on December 27, 1958 (Fig. 1.3). Al, Jack, and Frans were taken to New Zealand's Scott Base on the south slope of Mount Erebus, about one mile from NAF McMurdo. There they were to spend the winter with several New Zealand personnel (Kiwis), including Arnie Heine, the New Zealander whom Al recruited to join the VLT team as an assistant glaciologist. John Russell was also bivouacked at Scott Base, but needed to be replaced because of an injury. Two other members of the VLT team, already at NAF McMurdo with the U.S. Navy support group, were Chief Petty

Figure 1.3. Naval Air Facility (NAF) McMurdo Station in the center background. In the foreground, the tanker USS *Nespelen* is anchored and icebound at the ice's edge. Captain Robert Falcon Scott's hut, his team's wintering-over location on "Hut Point," is seen on the peninsula below NAF McMurdo.

Figure 1.4. Jack Weihaupt (foreground); on top of SnoCat: Bert Crary (left) and Buck Wilson (right). Photo taken when Jack, Al, and Frans joined Crary's traverse on the lower reaches of the Skelton Glacier.

Officer Warren Jackman, the Navy photographer who asked to accompany the VLT team for a portion of the journey in order to provide a photograph record of the team's ascent of the Skelton Glacier, and Tommy Baldwin, who would replace John Russell as the VLT mechanic.

Frans, Jack, Al, and Trevor Hatherton, a New Zealand glaciologist, were next flown by U.S. Navy VX-6 helicopter from NAF McMurdo south over the Ross Ice Shelf just east of the Transantarctic Mountains to join Albert P. (Bert) Crary's returning traverse (Fig. 1.4). Frans, Jack, and Al joined Crary's party for the last week of their traverse, and familiarized themselves with the SnoCats; sleds; seismic, gravity, and magnetic instrumentation; and glaciological techniques and equipment, all of which were to be turned over to the VLT team upon termination of Crary's traverse. Familiarization also with the risks associated with crevasses in the vicinities of glaciers and in the continental ice sheet would prove its worth. Bert, Chief Scientist for the United States in Antarctica, was long experienced in polar scientific exploration. Having set out from Little America on the Ross Ice Shelf, the Crary traverse ascended the Skelton Glacier to the eastern margin of the Victoria Land Plateau in the footsteps of Sir Vivian Fuchs' 1957–1958 British Commonwealth Transantarctic

Figure 1.5. Jack with a New Zealand dog team on the Ross Ice Shelf near Scott Base.

Expedition. On the high plateau, Bert's team collected seismic, gravity, and glaciological data that would provide a scientific jumping-off point for the VLT team.

While with the Crary team, Jack, Al, and Frans were integrated into the daily routine of traverse life and work, and dealing with some of the rigors, including the dangers posed in a heavily crevassed area. Crary's group, along with Jack, Al, and Frans, returned to NAF McMurdo on January 31, 1959. On hand for their arrival was Bill, who had now been approved by the VLT team to join them.

Once they returned from the Crary traverse, Frans, Jack, and Al were bivouacked at New Zealand's Scott Base on Ross Island, at the foot of volcanic Mount Erebus. From there, the VLT team made preparations for its journey in the spring. They promptly got their quarters organized, also helping the Kiwis with chores, such as cleaning, disposing of honey buckets, carpentry, repairs, and, eventually, preparing for the coming summer's VLT. They familiarized themselves further with the SnoCats, their engines, tracks, pontoons, radios, five-ton sleds, scientific instrumentation, and the maintenance and repair of the equipment, including the seismic, gravity, and magnetic instruments, and the glaciological equipment including a ramsonde, a device used for measuring snow hardness. Learning to operate the crevasse detector was a main concern, given the sensitivity of the device. Since it was mounted on the front of one of the SnoCats, that vehicle was dubbed *Detector Cat,* and would normally be operated by Al and Arnie. A second SnoCat housed the seismic, gravity, magnetic, and other geophysical instrumentation, and was dubbed *Seismo. Seismo* was normally operated by Jack and Frans. The third SnoCat was the vehicle in which food was stored, prepared, and consumed during the team's three daily meals, and was dubbed *Mess Cat. Mess Cat* was normally operated by Bill and whoever might be riding with him on a given day.

Al and Arnie ran glaciological trials, digging snow pits, operating the ramsonde, and practicing the techniques they would use on the traverse, some of which were techniques developed by Charles Swithinbank and others on the Norwegian-British-Swedish Antarctic Expedition of 1949–1952. During the winter, Al also taught himself celestial navigation, while Frans arranged for a Navy demolition team to detonate charges for seismic sounding trials. Jack, a lover of dogs, familiarized himself with dog teams and dog sledding (Fig. 1.5). With interest also in learning Morse code, Frans taught himself the technique with the help of the Navy radio operators at NAF McMurdo. Two types of radios would be used by the VLT team, a U.S. Army ANGRC19 and an ANGRC9. Not sufficiently powerful for voice communication with NAF McMurdo from the high plateau, it would be necessary to communicate by Morse code. During the winter, a considerable amount of time was devoted to assembling and packing food and other provisions—some of which would be kept frozen until the start of the traverse and then transported on a metal rack located on the top of Mess Cat's cab. Finally, a Navy physician at NAF McMurdo gave a first aid course for team members, providing a very complete first aid kit, and an ample supply of morphine and other medications.

Prior to the VLT team departure, Al did a reconnaissance of the coast of the Transantarctic Mountains on a U.S. Navy Squadron VX6 P2V flight, scouting for potential exits from the polar plateau. The mountainous coast and the extensive crevassing of the numerous glaciers confirmed that exiting from the Victoria Land Plateau was unlikely to be possible during or at the end of the traverse, and that if the team should succeed in reaching the western foothills of the Transantarctic Mountains, it would most likely be necessary to evacuate them by ski-equipped R4D aircraft or by helicopter to a waiting ice breaker.

Knowing little of what lay ahead, the VLT team was tasked with departing Scott Base in October 1959, in the Austral Springtime in Antarctica. The traverse was to retrace Captain Robert Falcon Scott's ill-fated route on the Ross Ice Shelf as far as the Skelton Glacier, then use the Skelton Glacier as Sir Vivian Fuchs had done on his now famous Commonwealth Transantarctic Expedition as a way from the Ross Shelf to the East Antarctic high plateau. This was the route used also by Bert Crary's traverse after departing Little America that year. The VLT team would then ascend the Skelton Glacier through the Transantarctic Mountains to the high Victoria Land Plateau. Thereafter, if all went well, the VLT was to explore as far as possible into unexplored Victoria Land, collecting as much seismic, gravity, magnetic, glaciological, and geological data as possible (Fig. 1.6). The seismic work that Frans and Jack would do involved an

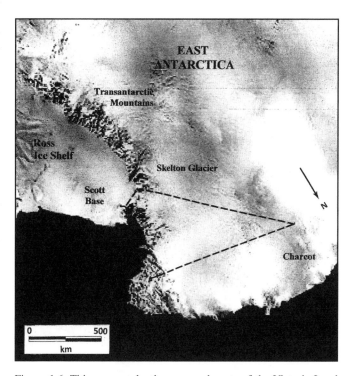

Figure 1.6. This map marks the proposed route of the Victoria Land Traverse from Scott Base, over the Ross Ice Shelf to the foot of the Skelton, then up the Skelton Glacier, and across the Victoria Land Plateau in the direction of Charcot. Should they locate the end point of the French Adélie Land Traverse of the year before, the team was then to head east toward the Ross Sea.

element of risk because it required the use of explosives. Some of the VLT team's colleagues had been killed or injured while doing this kind of seismic work. Al and Arnie were to gather glaciological data at points along the VLT route in an effort to reveal Antarctic climatic variations of the historic and prehistoric past. The first goal of the VLT team would be to traverse west over the Victoria Land Plateau more than 1,500 km to the end point of the French oversnow traverse, the Adélie Land Traverse (ALT), which had penetrated inland from their station at Dumont d'Urville on the coast in 1958–1959.

Lying at an elevation of more than 3,000 m, little was known about Victoria Land—the thickness of its massive continental ice sheet, the rate of annual snowfall and accumulation, the gravitational variations generated from the continental rocks far beneath the ice, its wavering magnetic field and wandering South Magnetic Pole, its seasonal atmospheric temperature variations and circulation, the possibility of polar life in the deep interior, and the geographic features, crevasses, valleys, mountains, and glaciers it might hold. From the end point of the ALT, should they find it, the VLT team was then to travel 1,000 km due east to the vicinity of the Tucker Glacier late in the season, there likely to be evacuated by helicopter to an icebreaker waiting in the Ross Sea. Unanticipated events would greatly compromise this plan and prevent this evacuation.

After the long winter of preparations for the VLT Bill, who had returned to the United States, flew from the United States back to New Zealand, then traveled from Christchurch on the U.S. Navy VX-6 Lockheed Constellation to join the VLT team, arriving at NAF McMurdo in late September. Jack, who had been injured in a crevasse fall on Mount Erebus, and evacuated to New Zealand, returned to Scott Base to rejoin the VLT team before its departure. The traverse would depart Scott Base in October, bound for the Skelton Glacier. Unable to be present at Scott Base at the time of departure, Claude and Taylor were later flown out to the team by a ski-equipped Navy R4D8 aircraft. Lou Roberts, who arrived still later, was flown out to the traverse by a Navy helicopter, joining the group shortly after it began its ascent of the Skelton Glacier.

Chapter 2

Scott Base to Skelton Inlet

The Tucker SnoCats were packed, the sleds were hitched, and the fuel tanks were full. A sizeable crowd of well-wishers assembled to see the Victoria Land Traverse depart New Zealand's Scott Base (Fig. 2.1). There was an abundance of good-natured ribbing and well-wishing by the Kiwis as the VLT team climbed aboard their SnoCats and started the engines. Detector and Seismo roared their readiness for the journey, *but*—when the starter was pressed on Mess Cat, it emitted—a click—a dull click! Dead battery! A chorus of hoots and hollers filled the frigid air. Another chorus of admonitions from the Kiwis emerged, questioning the probability of completing such a journey.

With Mess Cat's battery replaced, the SnoCats lurched, hit their stride, and headed south over the Ross Ice Shelf as the Kiwis looked on and photographed the departure (Fig. 2.2). It was 0945, Friday, October 16, 1959. There was a solidly overcast sky, gentle wind, and a temperature of –20 °C (–4 °F), with Detector in the lead, Seismo second, and Mess Cat bringing up the rear. The VLT track would take the traverse across the Ross Ice Shelf to Skelton Inlet at the foot of the Skelton Glacier. The glacier would be the highway, enabling the VLT to make the 3,000-m ascent from the Ross Ice Shelf, 175 km to the polar plateau.

The first week of travel found the VLT team establishing its daily routine, further familiarizing itself with the equipment, each team member assuming his unique responsibilities, and each integrating his modus with that of the other members of the team. The vehicles tracked pontoons, attached to large leaf springs, made for uncomfortable travel in rough sastrugi-ridden terrain. The greatest comfort could be found in the driver's seat, where support was provided by the seat and steering wheel. Other niches offered fewer mitten-holds in rough, tumbling terrain. Initially the snow surface was smooth and comfortable over the Ross Ice Shelf, and the driving manageable, but within days the snow surface gave way to hard *sastrugi*, waves of wind-compacted snow. The team was to learn that this would be the normal condition on the high plateau, 'though there waves of sastrugi would be much higher, much rougher, and ubiquitous. Beneath the sastrugi lay the ice mass of the Ross Ice Shelf, the size of France, nourished both by the valley glaciers flowing from the Transantarctic Mountains to the west, and by each season's

snow accumulation. En route to Skelton Inlet, the glaciologists measured the snow accumulation and ice movement from bamboo stakes left by Crary's team.

By 1900 the evening of the first day, the team had traveled 61 km (38 miles), the SnoCats averaging 6.5 km per hour. At the first station on the ice (Fig. 2.3), the team assembled in Mess Cat, comparing experiences, debriefing, and enjoying the first dinner on "The Ice." Not altogether a smooth affair for Bill, who was learning where pots and pans were stored, how the stove operated, and where the food stuffs were hidden. All in all, the team's first meal on "The Ice" went well. The food and conversation were pleasant and energizing. The team looked forward to the next day's travel, and to a very long adventure on the high plateau.

The team members' daily routines were quickly established. Next came the need to establish a travel and scientific observations routine. It was agreed that the team would have "travel days" and "station days." Travel days were essential, of course, to get from the Victoria Land Plateau, to the ALT end station near the Southern Ocean, and thence eastward to the end of the VLT in the foothills of the Transantarctic Mountains. Station days too were essential, for the collection of scientific data, to determine the thickness of the continental ices sheet, the land topography beneath the ice, and the glaciological nature of the centuries of accumulated snow. It was agreed also that there would be equal numbers of travel days and station days, and that travel days would alternate with station days. The morning of each travel day began with each team member readying for the day's activities, followed by Detector's departure along the day's predetermined route. After the first hour of travel, Detector would plant a trail-marker pole in the snow surface for Seismo to find at its first stop, and radio Seismo that it was moving on. Seismo, with Mess Cat trailing, began its first hour of travel for the day as Detector proceeded to its second stop one hour away, planting again a trail flag for Seismo to find and retrieve for later travel days. This "leap frog" routine, which began on the first day of travel, continued for the entire traverse. Throughout the traverse, radio contact would be maintained between SnoCats on travel days to keep team members informed about conditions, equipment failures,

Figure 2.1. The VLT team about to depart Scott Base. Center, front to back: Frans, Arnie, and Jack bid farewell to their Kiwi friends at Scott Base.

and obstacles that might be encountered. So went all the travel days, except for equipment failures and crevasse interruptions.

Scientific observations were made, however, on travel days as well as on station days. Elevations were determined at each travel day stop, the stops usually at 3–5 km separations, where trail flags had been left as markers. Atmospheric pressure variations were recorded, gravity observations were made at each such trail flag stop, and readings of Earth's magnetic field variations were taken. This information would provide a continuous 2,400-km profile across Victoria Land of seismic, gravity, magnetic, glaciological, elevation, atmospheric, and isotope variations, if the VLT team should achieve its final goal.

The second day of travel, Saturday, October 17, was clear and sunny, −25 °C (−13 °F), with little wind. Detector departed at 1000, scouting ahead. An hour later, after a radio message from Detector, Seismo and Mess Cat followed. By 1730, and after a two-hour search, the site of Crary's Station 86 was sighted. While searching for the trail flag of Crary's Station 86, the temperature began to drop, and the rough sastrugi caused the failure of one of the crevasse detector booms.

On the morning of the third day, the sky was clear, sunny, and −32 °C (−25.6 °F), again with little or no wind. It began with repairs to the wooden crevasse detector boom and measurements of the snow accumulation and strain line marker Crary

Figure 2.2. Kiwis saying goodbye as the VLT team departs from Scott Base. Cameras ready, it was a historic occasion with, clearly, some doubt in the air.

Figure 2.3. The VLT team's first station on the Ross Ice Shelf. Left to right: Detector, Seismo, and Mess Cat.

had left at Station 86. The work completed by lunch, the traverse resumed at 1430, the wind steadily increasing to 30 knots (34.5 mph) (Fig. 2.4). Reminiscent of Captain Robert Falcon Scott's last days, where he and the remaining men of his Terra Nova Expedition perished in 1912, wind and blizzard threatened. Our encampment was only a few miles from Scott's final resting place, and by 2130, the surface wind was blowing hard. As Bill washed pots and pans, the "hot" water with detergent froze. The traverse completed 14 km (8.5 miles) before stopping for the day—only 2,348 km to go!

By morning, snow had accumulated around the SnoCats' engines, making it necessary to use the Herman-Nelson heater mounted on Seismo's sled to melt the snow, heat Seismo's oil pan, and start its engine. Jumper cables to Detector and Mess Cat then got the traverse going. Cold, clear, and still windy, with snow drifts around the vehicles, Detector got under way at 1100. The VLT team drove until 1730 when an unannounced Navy R4D from NAF McMurdo landed at the team's location with two new members of the team: Claude Lorius from France and Al Taylor arrived with mail. Claude and Taylor reported that the plane had

Figure 2.4. Strong wind on the Ross Ice Shelf.

made a run to the head of the Skelton Glacier on the high plateau before landing at this location. Up there the winds were strong at more than 30 knots (34.5 mph) and the temperature −41.5 °C (−43 °F). The R4D took off, and the traverse was resumed until 1900 that day. That evening there were nine assembled around the dinner table in Mess Cat, and a lively discussion ensued about the days that lay ahead.

On Tuesday morning, October 20, there was a 15–20 knot (17–23 mph) wind, and snow had once more drifted 'round the vehicles. Up at 0830, nine assembled for breakfast as the SnoCat engines purred and warmed. Detector left at 1040 for Crary's Station 57, as strong winds and blowing snow reduced the visibility. Unfamiliar with these conditions, Taylor, while outside the 'Cat, was shaken by his inability to see his team around him, or to find his way back to the 'Cats. An experience familiar to most polar explorers, thereafter Taylor stayed "close to home." Taylor's experience was remembered as the days went on; others of the team had become fearful when visibility diminished in the blowing snow—with good reason as crevasses now were all around us.

The next morning, with heavy drifting once more streaming around the vehicles, a scattered overcast and a 20–30 knot (23–35 mph) wind greeted the team as we emerged from a deep night's sleep. Frans, Al, Arnie, and Claude ventured out to re-measure the strain line at Station 57. Following breakfast, and once more on our way, it became difficult to maintain a heading with the reduced visibility. The VLT team traveled only 8 km (5 miles) that day, spending the late day in Mess Cat discussing again the challenges that lay ahead, over Bill's servings of hot buttered rum. That evening, as with each evening on the traverse, the VLT team met its radio schedule with NAF McMurdo. Using voice communication in the early days, Morse code became the only means of communication when the weather deteriorated and as distances from NAF McMurdo increased. Frans sent and received the Morse code messages. Learning from that evening's radio message that Lou Roberts, our topographic engineer, would soon join us caused some concern. The team complement would stand at ten. Sleeping arrangements and seating at meals would be something of a challenge, except for the fact that Jackman would be evacuated when the traverse reached the head of the glacier.

On Thursday, October 22, Frans woke the crew at 0745, and the vehicles were under way by 0945. A thoroughly miserable day, wind and blowing snow and an overcast sky compromised the triangulation needed for positioning. The nearby Transantarctic Mountains could not be seen, and magnetic compasses were of little use because of the VLT's nearness to the magnetic South Pole, which lay, ironically, on the Victoria Land Plateau *north* of our location. The traverse drove until 1600, making only 24 km (15 miles) that day. On Friday, a better day, Detector set out at 0940 over a smooth snow surface. An hour later, Seismo and Mess Cat followed.

The next day, Saturday, October 24, one week into the journey, the snow surface improved, there was no whiteout, and the sky was clear. With little or no wind and −35 °C (−31 °F),

Detector departed at 1000. The other 'Cats followed an hour later, arriving at Crary's Station 59 at 1300. The strain line re-measured, the traverse continued until 1600, having made 16 km (10 miles). About to make the last station stop at 1800, an unannounced VX-6 Otter aircraft passed low overhead. Seismo and Mess Cat stopped, making their scientific observations as the Otter approached Detector a mile or so ahead. For those riding in Detector, an unsettling sight appeared as the Otter made its approach. It came in at a very low altitude. Appearing to be much too low, the plane seemed strangely to be flying into or below the snow surface, as through there was an unseen valley in the horizon! What Detector had been experiencing was light refraction caused by an atmospheric inversion, temperature stratification in the air. Then, as the plane approached Detector, its propeller mixed the air, destroying the cold stratified layer, restoring the reality of the horizon. The Otter landed safely in a swirl of snow as the "valley" disappeared! A helicopter, which we had not seen, also landed, bringing with it the long expected Rolligon, the rolling fuel transporter that, at NSF's request, Jack had evaluated the year before when he visited the factory in Clintonville, Wisconsin. The rolling fuel transporter was a new device—two huge rubber tires into which fuel was pumped. Provided also to evaluate fuel transport in harsh polar conditions, and to be used potentially by the military in the Arctic, the Rolligon would be towed by Jack and Frans' Seismo along with Seismo's five-ton sled. Each Rolligon tire held 450 gallons of fuel, eliminating the need to carry many more of the heavy 55-gallon steel fuel drums on already overloaded sleds. The Rolligon had not been used in polar conditions previously, so this would be the first opportunity to evaluate its effectiveness in a cold and harsh environment. The Rolligon was unhooked from the helicopter and hitched to Seismo, between the 'Cat and its sled (Fig. 2.5).

And, of course, there were almost daily happenings, bumps and bruises that are unavoidable, from the work and from the "tossing" vehicles as they rumbled over the sastrugi. This day Arnie was driving Mess Cat, making a turn to park alongside Detector, when he inadvertently bumped Mess Cat's sled into Detector's sled. Frans and Arnie, both visibly upset, scowled at one another. In Arnie's defense, he had asked for guidance before making the maneuver, but no one was available, as everyone was busy with several tasks. As always, the issue faded into the sun-filled night. At dinner, there was a cheery mood, a feeling that the traverse team had a very good day, due primarily to the good weather and the arrival of the Otter and the helicopter. It was always good to get a visit from the outside world. After re-measuring the strain line, everyone retired to Mess Cat, enjoying hot tea, coffee, hot chocolate, or, in some cases, a brandy. Conversation was animated and delightful.

On Sunday morning, Detector departed at 0945. Seismo and Mess Cat followed. At the first trail flag stop, Mess Cat's steering connecting rod broke. Tommy quickly began repairs as Detector's crew reconnoitered for Crary's nearby Station 60, which they failed to find. By 1700, now skirting signs of crevasses,

Figure 2.5. Rolligon hitched behind Seismo and in front of its sled. The orange box mounted on the towbar ahead of the Rolligon is a tool box that was abundantly used on the traverse.

some bridged and others not, they gave up the search, returning to that night's camp, near the foot of the Skelton Glacier where it flows into the Ross Ice Shelf. Now 320 km (200 miles) from Scott Base, the area was ideal crevasse country. Perhaps the greatest danger faced here, and eventually on the high plateau, was crevasses concealed by snow bridges. The team, fully conscious of the challenges faced by explorers before them, such as Shackleton, Scott, Amundsen, Mawson, and Byrd, retired to sleeping bags at 2000, anticipating the ascent of the Skelton Glacier, now only a few kilometers to the west.

Up at 0715, the Herman-Nelson heater was again fired up; the engines of Detector and Mess Cat had failed to start. With Seismo started, Detector headed off at 1030, the others at 1130. After 16 km

(10 miles) Jack spotted the barrel at Crary's Station 60. Detector remeasured the strain line, avoiding signs of hidden crevasses.

Resuming travel toward Skelton Inlet, the team was surprised again to hear the sound of aircraft engines. Two VX-6 helicopters arrived at 1230. The visits by VX-6 aircraft at the beginning of the journey appeared to be due to the squadron's desire to see the VLT—while it was still around—before it disappeared up-glacier, and into the wild unknown. This time the helicopters were there to fly a reconnaissance up the Skelton Glacier (Fig. 2.6), to scout the route that might offer the best chance of success for the VLT team to avoid crevasses. A wonderful advantage not enjoyed by Scott as he struggled up the nearby Beardmore Glacier or during Roald Amundsen's journey up the Axel Heiberg Glacier in

Figure 2.6. Frans and Al depart by helicopter on a recon of the Skelton Glacier.

Figure 2.7. Al, Frans (foreground), Taylor (red parka), Jackman (blue parka), and Arnie (on Detector Cat) at Crary's cache. The foot of the Skelton Glacier is in the background.

their races to the Pole, the helicopters were a blessing, saving time and maybe even lives.

Ed Thiel, Ed Robinson, John Russell, and others had hitched a helicopter ride to visit the VLT. All good friends, they were welcomed with open arms upon arrival. Frans and Al went on the recon of the glacier while the rest assembled in Mess Cat with, again, hot tea and conversation. Ed Thiel and Ed Robinson, veterans of previous traverses, had advice to offer about the dangers that lay ahead. This was the last time any of us would see Ed Thiel. One year and thirteen days later, November 8, 1961, while Jack was en route to the South Pole on another seismic and gravity project, Ed perished in the crash of a Navy P2V on takeoff from Wilkes Station. After that, Ed's wife Pat, who was pregnant with their first child, moved in with Jack's wife Audrey in Madison, Wisconsin.

The next day Detector was under way at 0930 and by noon had found Crary's Station 64, along with a food cache left by Crary's team near Teal Island. It is a tradition of polar exploration that returning expeditions leave caches of unused food and supplies as they near their home bases. The caches are intended for

Figure 2.8. Claude happily going through the cache left by Crary's team near the bottom of the Skelton Glacier. Boxes of candy bars at his right—and on the snow.

later explorers that might be in need. Detector, ~8 km (5 miles) ahead, was the first to arrive at the cache. Shortly thereafter an Otter arrived, again unannounced, bringing four drums of fuel and some very welcome fresh food. The Otter took off before Seismo and Mess Cat arrived at the cache. Delighted with the discovery of Crary's cache, the VLT team rummaged through the boxes (Figs. 2.7 and 2.8), leaving for later explorers what they would not need. The team then loaded the 55-gallon fuel drums onto sleds. The Otter had brought fresh eggs, scrambled for a late lunch–early dinner, with fresh tomatoes, onions, and a dessert of fresh oranges. Frans connected his converter to a tape recorder, and Beethoven, likely for the first time ever, filled the polar air of Antarctica's Ross Ice Shelf. The team relaxed in unlikely splendor.

Al and Arnie left ~2030 to do re-measurements at Crary's Station 64. Out until 0500 the next morning re-surveying a network of movement and accumulation stakes, Arnie spotted a small but lurking crevasse as they drove halfway between Teal Island and Fishtail Point. Al hadn't seen it as the SnoCat's pontoon skirted the opening. We knew there would be many more. Fractures in glaciers and ice sheets caused by the stresses of ice movement over subglacial rock topography, crevasses are frequently concealed by snow bridges caused by blowing snow.

Most often structurally too weak to support vehicles and even humans, most snow bridges were found by the traverse team to collapse easily, disabling SnoCats and sometimes an inattentive member of the team. Bert Crary's team had marked a safe path up the glacier with trail flags the year before. They proved, however, to be deceptive as the glacier had moved in the interim, leading the VLT team sometimes into severely crevassed areas. With the exception of Arnie, none of the team had experience with crevasses. Frans, Jack, and Jackman, reconnoitering the camp that evening, spotted dozens more—harbingers of what was to come once on the glacier.

The sleepy conversation next morning was about crevasses, as the team broke its fast. Common at the foot of glaciers, crevasses are common too at the bases of nunataks and mountains, therefore abundant on the margins of the glacier. Seismo's heavy Rolligon, intended for quite a different purpose, became a rolling crevasse detector, destroying numerous small snow bridges that had gone otherwise unseen. Ironically, and disturbingly, the Rolligon, towed *behind* Seismo, did its crevasse detecting *after* Seismo had crossed the waiting predators. Our wariness now well in hand, and at the foot of the Skelton Glacier, the team was prepared for its assault on the glacier (Fig. 2.9).

Figure 2.9. Bill in Mess Cat, ready to head up-glacier.

Chapter 3

The Skelton Glacier—Crevasse country

The Skelton Glacier winds through the Transantarctic Mountains 175 km (110 miles) to the East Antarctic high plateau. In 1958, Sir Edmund Hillary ascended the Skelton Glacier, laying a supply cache at the head of the glacier in support of Sir Vivian Fuchs' Commonwealth Transantarctic Expedition. Fuchs' team had departed Shackleton Base on the Weddell Sea on November 24, 1957, arriving at the U.S. South Pole Station on January 19, 1958. Hillary continued on to South Pole Station, met Fuchs and then guided Fuchs' team to the head of the Skelton Glacier, then to the Ross Ice Shelf, and on to Scott Base, arriving on March 2, 1958. In 1958, Bert Crary's team, departing from Little America, climbed the Skelton Glacier, then headed due west some 560 km (350 miles) onto the high plateau, preliminary to the VLT (Fig. 3.1).

Wednesday, October 28, the VLT team found itself camped in Skelton Inlet at the foot of the Skelton Glacier. The day was clear with little wind and a temperature of −35 °C (−31 °F). The days before the ice surface had been wind polished with small dimples, making walking treacherous (Fig. 3.2). But this day was different, enabling the VLT team to work until 0500, as Arnie and Al slept until 1300 after their excursion of the night before below the ramparts of the glacier's mountains (Fig. 3.3). Lingering at breakfast, with crevasses in the backs of team members' minds, the group exchanged views on politics and morality in politics and then turned attention back to the crevasse field in which the VLT team now found itself. Attention then turned to the crevasse detector. Consisting of four wooden booms attached to the front of Detector, each beam had mounted on it an aluminum pan acting as an electrode. The aluminum pans, resting on the snow surface ahead of the SnoCat, were connected electrically to a detecting device inside Detector. An electric current transmitted from one of the pans, through the snow, to the other pans created an electric field in the surface snow beneath the pans. If the field was interrupted by, for example an air space—a crevasse, an alarm was triggered inside the SnoCat warning of the presence of crevasses. The VLT team found that the presence of snow bridges over crevasses often had the effect of compromising the detection of a crevasse since the electric field was then conducted through

the snow bridge and therefore not interrupted. As a result, the crevasse detector most often failed to work.

The crevasse detector was nevertheless activated, and team members pursued their tasks around the camp before the day's travel. The crevasse detector once more failed to operate, so several members of the team roped up and probed with aluminum poles ahead of Detector. The poles, frequently penetrating snow bridges that concealed crevasses, worked satisfactorily. So did feet, legs, and, more often, a team member falling through a snow bridge waist high or more. At 1500 the traverse headed up the glacier, soon running off the wind-polished ice (Fig. 3.2). The glacial ice was now snow covered, making it difficult to see crevasses. Near the end of the day's travel, the crevasse detector momentarily beeped a warning, flashing a red light and sounding a bell. It warned of a crevasse five meters ahead. This was the first time the crevasse detector functioned properly. Nonetheless, its importance was confirmed. A very large crevasse, capable of swallowing an entire SnoCat, lay just beneath the snow. Had the crevasse not been detected, there was a good chance that Detector might have been lost and, potentially, the life of a VLT member.

Making 18.4 km (11.5 miles), the VLT team ended its first day on the glacier just below Bareface Bluff. The mountains emerging now around the team were reminders not only of the unforgiving nature of this land, but of the beauty of Antarctica. Stark beauty would be everywhere before the journey's end. At dinner that evening, everyone was crevasse conscious. Tommy, a young man of considerable sensitivity and wisdom, shared with the team that "whenever the SnoCat takes a dip, my ass puckers up!" Bill, sensitive to Tommy's observation, put a safety rope from Mess Cat to its sled, and became light footed whenever outside "his" Mess Cat. Jackman, upset by the day's happenings, began grumbling about dinner, complaining that he was still hungry. Bill had not prepared enough food; the cold had burned too many calories.

Thursday morning, October 29, a strong *katabatic* wind blew down the glacier. Frans missed breakfast that morning. He had been trying to repair the crevasse detector. His attempts had not gone well. "Good God, we've only been out twelve days, and have three more months to go!" At 1030, he and Al left in

Detector to go on a crevasse detector test run. Upon their return, frustrated and still not in good humor, Frans resolved that we should resume our trek up-glacier with or without the crevasse detector. After Detector left, Jack, who was saving his warmest clothes for later in the journey, came down with chills and a temperature of 101 °F. Feeling under the weather, he nonetheless piled into Seismo and, with Mess Cat bringing up the rear, departed at 1130. Twin Rocks was ~48 km (30 miles) away. We should make it by that evening. Arriving near Twin Rocks, Jack's temperature was down to 100.4 °F, although Arnie, Al, Jackman, and Bill now complained of not feeling well, perhaps the result of exposure to our visitors on the 27th. This capped the dinner conversation, leading uncomfortably to talk of physical ailments, surgeries and, disturbingly, death. We all agreed it was the lurk-ing crevasses that had set the tone, but we all blamed Jack, who had been the first to become ill! Arnie noted that those who wintered over at Scott Base frequently came down with colds after visitors arrived at the end of the winter season.

Pressure ridges now loomed large across the trail ahead, often revealing 2-m-wide crevasses. In the afternoon, Seismo's rear pontoon broke through the snow bridge of a 2-m-wide crevasse, our first crevasse accident (Figs. 3.4 and 3.5). Jack, Arnie, and Tommy quickly worked to get Seismo free. Mess Cat's sled was detached; then Seismo's sled was detached. Mess Cat next backed up to Seismo and, straddling the crevasse, attached a length of cable, to the front of Seismo. With Jack in Seismo's driver's seat, and Tommy in Mess Cat's, they succeeded in pulling Seismo free.

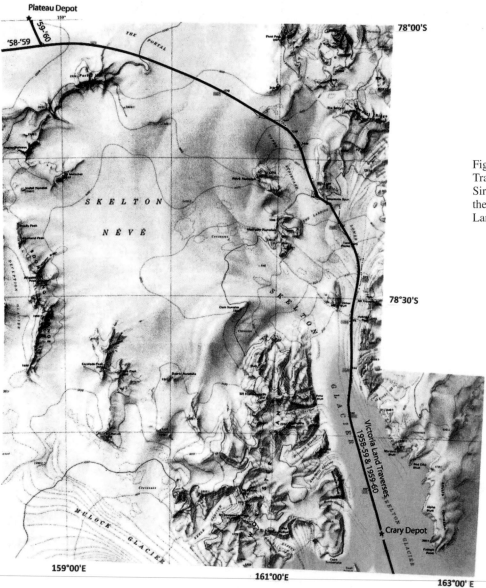

Figure 3.1. The Skelton Glacier in the Transantarctic Mountains, the routes of Sir Edmund Hillary, Sir Vivian Fuchs, the Crary Traverse, and the Victoria Land Traverse of 1959–1960.

Figure 3.2. Wind-polished ice at the foot of the Skelton glacier.

The Victoria Land Traverse team's first encounter with a crevasse, and first attempt at SnoCat extraction, was an event that became the format for later such occasions. A steering tie-rod end on Seismo had broken in the crevasse accident, and discussion ensued about whether a fix could be jury-rigged, because there was no replacement part. Tommy, Jack, and Frans began working on a fix. Once finished, they hitched Seismo to its Rolligon and sled (Fig. 3.6), and Seismo was ready to resume. Jack placed a red trail flag to mark the crevasse. Very shortly thereafter, one of Detector's sled runners broke through another snow bridge, damaging the runner. Another fix was made.

Jack's cold, now presumed to be strep throat, continued, as did his fever. There was discussion regarding whether he should be airlifted back to NAF McMurdo, but he would have none of it. Conceding to the cold, Jack put on his best parka. Warmer now, and no longer chilled, within a day he was well again. That evening during the scheduled radio contact with NAF McMurdo, Frans requested parts for the broken steering tie-rod end. The next day, two helicopters and two Otter aircraft would fly out

Figure 3.3. The southwest boundary of the lower reaches of the Skelton Glacier.

Figure 3.4. Seismo has the first crevasse accident. Smith and Jackman taking photographs.

to the team's position to deliver parts, and to provide a recon up the glacier. At dinner the talk was all about crevasses. In the days ahead the VLT team would need to be vigilant because many of the crevasses would be concealed by snow bridges. After dinner Frans put on the casette of the first movement of Beethoven's Fifth Symphony. Unreal—Beethoven on the Skelton—we listened pensively as the wind blew—well into the night.

The next morning the VLT team was advised by radio that the aircraft scheduled to our location were grounded because of the intense winds. With a whiteout created by the winds, with the reduced visibility here in crevasse country, with crevasses now all around us, and with the need for spare parts, it was decided to continue at this station for another day. A recon up the glacier next day, Saturday, October 31, would put us in much better stead to continue our ascent. The day was devoted to checking vehicles and sleds for signs of weakness or damage, and for consolidating our field notes and scientific data. Dinner this wind-blown night was at 1730. Afterward Arnie requested that Frans provide another evening of musical reverie. Frans selected Mozart's "Jupiter" symphony, as Arnie broke out his small stash of New Zealand Navy rum. The assemblage, if you can picture it, became quietly absorbed. Ignoring the howling winds that rocked Mess Cat in tune with the lilt of classical crescendo, it was a memorable interlude. Quiet next settled on the night until—the team now joined in with singing!

On Halloween morning, October 31, Frans attempted again to jury-rig the broken steering tie-rod end so that we could travel. Once more unsuccessful, he attempted radio contact with Scott Base at 0900, to confirm delivery of spare parts, but

Figure 3.5. Seismo's rear pontoons collapsed the snow bridge over this crevasse. The challenges of extracting the SnoCat are apparent.

Figure 3.6. Seismo's Rolligon and sled. The imposing mountains grow in size and stature up-glacier.

that too was unsuccessful. We could not raise them, nor did they call us, nor did the helicopters come. With low-lying clouds, the wind now was barely blowing. The weather warmed to temperatures above zero, an indication that a storm was on the way. It snowed that afternoon.

November 1 was windy, with blowing snow, and mostly cloudy. Still no helicopters. We had to get the traverse moving, so Tommy and Frans continued to work diligently on a fix for the steering tie-rod end. After breakfast Tommy, Claude, and Bill, who lived in Mess Cat, asked everyone to leave the vehicle

so that they could do some house cleaning. Bill shaved, generating humorous commentary, and brushed his teeth. Tommy and Frans repaired the tie-rod end provisionally—it worked a little bit—enough to allow slow travel. Crevasses now were everywhere. Probing revealed a threatening crevasse beneath a snow bridge just ahead on the trail. With Tommy's help, Jack lowered himself into the crevasse. He estimated the crevasse to be 2 m (6 ft.) wide, 18 m (60 ft.) deep, and several hundred meters long. Had one of the SnoCats fallen in, it is likely that it would have sustained considerable damage. By morning,

Figure 3.7. Nature, never resting, begins to build a new snow bridge. By evening the crevasse was again concealed.

Figure 3.8. A strong downslope glacier (*katabatic*) wind coated Jack with blowing snow as he scouted for crevasses.

wind would sweep the crevasse's edges (Fig. 3.7), beginning a new snow bridge.

Monday morning, November 2, the sky was cloudy and windy with heavy blowing snow, but a warm –10 °C (14 °F). Again, no helicopters and no travel. Jack fell through a snow bridge while scouting around the camp, sinking to his waist (Fig. 3.8). Stuggling out, he marked it with a red trail flag. Then Al broke out his gin, and Jack produced vermouth—Martinis in hand, they toasted all at dinner.

A strong wind blew on Tuesday, November 3—30 knots (34.5 mph), and the temperature again was warm, –16 °C (–3.2 °F). By 1115, Bill and Tommy filled the gas can for the cook stove in an unrelenting wind as blowing snow threatened white-out. In conditions difficult to navigate while on foot, helicopters nonetheless appeared down-glacier, two orange dots above the blowing snow struggling to negotiate the katabatic wind. Lieu-

tenant Colonel Merle "Skip" Dawson peered from the window as pilot Lieutenant Commander Edgar "Al" Potter set the chopper down (Fig. 3.9). Skip wondered how the Rolligon was working. Jack and Frans' experience thus far had been good with the Rolligon. While it was a superb crevasse detector, it served well also as a fuel transporter. Skip confided that the VLT team was on a "God-forsaken" mission, and that he and his crew would provide all the help they could.

The second helicopter arrived, taking Al on a recon flight to the head of Skelton Glacier. Al returned, reporting that he'd seen scores of large crevasses. George Toney, on board that helicopter, assisted in driving trail flags into the surface as the helicopter flew low, in an attempt to mark a route through crevasse fields. The last addition to the VLT team, Lou Roberts (Fig. 3.10), was aboard one of the helicopters, and now assumed his duties with the team. The delivery of spare parts, tie-rod ends, mail, and

Figure 3.9. Lieutenant Colonel Skip Dawson (left); Lieutenant Commander Edgar A. ("Al") Potter (right).

Figure 3.10. Lou joins the team.

fresh food was also most welcome. The tie-rod end was quickly repaired as the helicopters departed, and Detector resumed travel up-glacier. Seismo and Mess Cat set out an hour later at 1525. That evening, at Crary Station 66, traverse work resumed. Taylor, Arnie, Al, and Lou ventured into a strong downslope wind to measure strain lines and movement stakes.

The next morning, re-stocked with parts, the VLT team got an early start, heading for the Skelton Neve (Fig. 3.1), the upper reaches of the glacier. Detector departed at 0850, Seismo and Mess Cat at 0950. The strong downslope wind and blowing snow continued, but, resupplied and anxious to make up lost time, good time was made until evening. Evening radio contact with NAF McMurdo contained a message for the Victoria Land Traverse team from Sir Edmund Hillary: "Good luck and bon voyage on a dangerous and historic undertaking." The team was elated!

Hillary's message, well wishes from this famous and bold adventurer, had an exhilarating effect on the now hard-pressed team. The winds continued to blow down-glacier and continued to cascade off the mountains. Crevasses had grown even more ubiquitous—they were everywhere. The SnoCats and sleds were especially vulnerable, given the heavy loads they carried. One or another of the vehicles and sleds fell into five crevasses in less than two hours. In the first, Detector's rear pontoons broke through a well-concealed and deep crevasse (Fig. 3.11). Now experienced in SnoCat extraction from the previous accident, the pontoons and crevasse were carefully inspected; then Mess Cat towed Detector free.

The VLT members proceeded now in tandem, arriving soon at another of Crary's trail markers from the year before when, once more, Detector broke through a sizeable snow bridge. This one, more serious than the last, required supporting the SnoCat somehow from beneath the dangling pontoons (Fig. 3.12). Frans and Jack roped up and, with the help of Tommy and Al, were lowered into the crevasse, well underneath the pontoons. Using ice axes to chop ledges into the crevasse's walls, they wedged bridging timbers to support the vehicle, and others to provide a ramp for Detector's extraction. As they did so, Detector creaked and slid, making clear the possibility that the 'Cat could drop deeper, with Frans and Jack beneath!

Figure 3.11. Detector, one hour in the lead, was unable to extract itself. Seismo and Mess Cat arrive to assist with Detector's extraction. Looking northeast.

Figure 3.12. The bridging timber that Frans and Jack installed under Detector Cat.

Now a matter of urgency, the work was pursued with diligence and energy. The surface crew did their job well, the entire team holding its collective breath. The work was done quickly as, with jerks and starts, Al drove Detector out of its predicament. Frans and Jack too were extricated. Jack marked the location of the crevasse (Fig. 3.13).

The glacier, as though insisting on its prerogatives, issued yet another warning—in fact three. It was not long before Detector crossed another hidden crevasse, and collapsed its bridge. Detector's rear pontoons again hung beneath the surface of the snow

(Fig. 3.14). Tommy drove Mess Cat around Detector to begin the now well-worn technique of SnoCat extraction when—Mess Cat's left rear pontoon broke through yet another snow bridge.

Two SnoCats now were in crevasses; only Seismo and its Rolligon and sled were free. Because Seismo too was at risk, the entire traverse might well find its conclusion here. Deciding to take the chance, Seismo was detached from its Rolligon and sled, attached to Mess Cat with a cable, and a successful attempt was made to extract Mess Cat from its predicament. Mess Cat, its gear in reverse, backed up to reposition itself with Seismo

Figure 3.13. Jack marks the crevasse with a trail flag.

Figure 3.14. Detector falls into another crevasse.

and Detector and unbelievably—and even more unacceptably—backed onto another snow bridge, broke through, and once again two of three SnoCats were inoperable. The traverse continued to be a risky and doubtful undertaking. Virtually immovable amid scores of unseen crevasses, the fate of the traverse would be determined by the team's resilience and resourcefulness. Jack and Frans took up the task of probing the snow surface ahead, each on a lengthy rope fixed to a SnoCat. Finding an abundance of crevasses, they marked each with trail flags. A Nitramon charge revealed the size, depth, and orientation of hidden cre-

vasses (Fig. 3.15). Then Al and Arnie continued probing and, when understandably fatigued, surrendered the metal poles to Claude, who was joined again by Frans. The team then turned its attention to extracting Detector and Mess Cat. Still a difficult and strenuous undertaking, Jack and Frans again installed bridging timbers underneath the vehicles. It was 1630 before the last SnoCat was freed. Enough for one day's travel and mindful of their predicament, the team stood silently together in the increasing wind and blowing snow. Though now exhausted, they confirmed their determination.

Figure 3.15. Snow bridge, discovered by probing, was blasted to reveal its size, depth, and orientation.

Chapter 4

Crevasse country to the high plateau

Following the episodes of equipment failures, no spare parts, and crevasse accidents, the Victoria Land Traverse team was nonetheless undaunted. A pretty hearty group, there was an unspoken recognition that the undertaking was a worthy one, and it was assumed by each subconsciously that every day we'd do our duty. We'd make it to the end. The Victoria Land Plateau of East Antarctica would be achieved, and the traverse would continue as planned, as long as the equipment, provisions, and the well-being of the team prevailed. There was the recognition too, and acceptance of the fact, that more challenges lay ahead, more crevasses would be encountered, disruptive failures of equipment were a certainty, and an occasional feather would be ruffled—unintentionally. The head of the glacier and Plateau Depot, a supply cache laid by VX-6, were still a long way away. We knew from Al's helicopter reconnaissance that crevasse fields remained to be crossed or somehow circumvented.

As dinner began Wednesday evening, there was little talk of what the team had been through, each of us reflecting on the happenings. But, then the mood began to change, some talking excitedly and adventurously with surprising good humor. Imaginations at work, some suggested ways to improve our chances, step up the pace, conserve fuel and provisions, and untried ways to avoid crevasses. Most of the ideas were wild and unworkable, but they confirmed that the group was alert and thinking. So we laughed a lot as Mozart filled the air.

The next morning the camp awoke to a breeze, clear sky, and temperature of –12 °C (10.4 °F). Breakfast was a cheerful affair, and surprisingly the crevasse detector showed signs of life again. So, Frans and Al roped up, tied themselves to one of the crevasse detector booms, and began probing the route ahead. The VLT team started out at 1000, toward Twin Rocks, which lay one mile ahead, and, unexpectedly, the crevasse detector beeped a flash. A crevasse was nearby. This, the second time the crevasse detector worked, would be the last. After today, it never found a crevasse again! Jack and Tommy set a Nitramon charge and blew the snow bridge, revealing another very large crevasse that easily would have disabled a SnoCat and its sled. Jack again roped up and, again with Tommy's help, explored another deep crevasse (Figs. 4.1 and 4.2). Had a SnoCat crossed the snow bridge, it would have been disastrous—the crevasse was a large one.

From the previous evening's radio contact with McMurdo, the team learned that two helicopters would again visit us on the glacier. They arrived with Al Potter piloting the first helicopter, with Skip Dawson by his side. The second helicopter, piloted by Buddy Krebs, brought George Toney and Jack Long from NAF McMurdo and with them a photo strip of the glacier made by

Figure 4.1. Jack's view from inside the crevasse.

Figure 4.2. The environment inside crevasses, particularly if covered by snow bridges, is quiescent, allowing for large ice crystals to form. Here, in the midst of potential danger, we once more find beauty in the glint of crystals from nature's creative brush.

a P2V the day before. The VLT team struggling up-glacier was clearly visible on it. Frans and Al then climbed aboard with Skip and Al Potter (Fig. 4.3) and did another recon to the head of the glacier. The helicopter piloted by Krebs, flew up-glacier just above the surface, while George and Jack Long again drove trail flags into the snow in an attempt to mark a safer trail than the one the traverse was taking.

The helicopters departed at 1500. This had been an important and successful day. A trail had been flagged, more spare parts had been delivered, and the VLT team again was prepared to be on its way. The temperature and wind were moderate, and fresh pie had been thoughtfully delivered, thanks to the helicopter crews. After a pie break, the VLT team resumed travel. Detector was now preceded by more aggressive probing for crevasses, as Al, Arnie, Claude, and Frans took turns probing—until the end of the travel day.

The traverse's nearness to the high plateau was exhilarating! A feeling of success was evident in the strides of the team. All were inwardly elated. The next morning Bill served a good breakfast of fresh eggs and bacon, flown in yesterday by the helicopters. Everyone was in good spirits. Jack confided that when he detonates an explosive charge in a snow bridge, when

the VX-6 pilots make more than expected visits, and when the team probes for crevasses, he sometimes thinks, "Kids playing at war." This brought chuckles of amusement, and then some nodding heads. After breakfast Frans probed for crevasses around the camp, finding a few with bridges strong enough to support both vehicles and sleds. Jack found a leak in Seismo's hydraulic system, which he fixed with Tommy's help. This travel day began more comfortably. Now near Twin Rocks, Detector slowly pulled away, with Seismo an hour behind (Fig. 4.4). It was a good day with no crevasse mishaps. Though the surface ice was rough, the scenery was spectacular. By 1830 the traverse had traveled 34 km (21 miles).

Saturday at breakfast Arnie remarked that he had slept only a few hours the past few nights due, he thought, to the stress of venturing through the crevasse fields. Post-breakfast began with Frans, Al, Arnie, and Taylor aboard Detector. They rolled out at 0900. Jack, Claude, and Lou in Seismo, and Tommy, Bill, and Jackman in Mess Cat, followed at 1010. The SnoCats tracked station flags left by Detector, leading over large ice ridges up through *The Portal* (Fig. 4.5), a region on the upper glacier that ran through and between sentry nunataks to Plateau Depot. The Portal was the entrance to the high plateau.

Figure 4.3. Al Potter and his helicopter were a welcome sight.

Figure 4.4. Seismo, now in the Skelton Neve (see Fig. 3.1), about to enter *The Portal*.

At dinner that evening the team assembled around the roughhewn table, and took pride in its achievement. The VLT team was, in fact, inside The Portal. Attention was diverted from feelings of good fortune, however, when Bill, preparing for his culinary responsibilities, took the Coleman gas tank outside Mess Cat for refilling. Returning it to its Mess Cat cooking shelf inside, it warmed. The gas expanded up through the filler cap, and overflowed. Frans, for some other purpose, had lit a match. The Coleman was now on fire! Everyone sat—staring in shock and amazement—until Jack, in no uncertain terms, suggested that the team evacuate the vehicle. A fire drill ensued. Being closest to the Coleman, and with pants ablaze, Bill threw the tank through the open door, diving after it. With flames now licking at his sleeves, Bill threw gobs of snow on his new responsibility. Al, cool in the face of Bill's disaster,

handed him a fire extinguisher, which Bill promptly passed to Jackman. Jackman, standing over Bill's now simmering folly, finished off the incident. There was, remarkably, little damage. The evening meal was still assured. Bill and Frans exchanged, in private, a few choice words. Pride in the team's arrival at The Portal overcame the incident.

The following day, Sunday, November 8, the weather had changed. It was much colder, −38 °C (−36.4 °F) and windy, with snow blowing at eye level (Fig. 4.6). The Herman-Nelson heater preheated the vehicles' engines. Close now to Plateau Depot, Detector moved out at 1030, with Seismo and Mess Cat close behind. The VLT team arrived at Plateau Depot, at the top of the Skelton Glacier, at 1230 (Fig. 4.7). Being at the top of the glacier was like being at the top of the world! Beautiful and awe inspiring, the peaks of the Transantarctic Mountains were behind

Figure 4.5. Entering *The Portal*. Plateau Depot is just ahead.

Figure 4.6. Jack. The katabatic winds were constant, coating one's beard with snow and ice.

and all around us. The Victoria Land polar plateau lay enticingly before us.

There was an abundance of supplies and provisions in the Plateau Depot cache (Fig. 4.8). As a result there was a great deal of work to do. The sleds had to be unloaded, repacked, and the cache supplies then loaded (Fig. 4.9). The afternoon was devoted to unloading, unpacking, repacking, and loading the SnoCats and the sleds. Each item was loaded in reverse order, depending upon when it was likely to be used. One ton of explosives was loaded onto Seismo's sled for Jack and Frans' seismic work. Drilling equipment and food were loaded, and twelve 55-gallon drums of fuel were muscled onto sleds. Some of the fuel was pumped from the drums directly into the SnoCat fuel tanks (Fig. 4.10). At six pounds per gallon, each drum weighed 135 kg (330 lbs), all

together a total of 1,620 kg (3,600 lbs) of fuel to be loaded and towed on the high plateau. Seismo hauled 8,100 kg (18,000 lbs), Detector hauled 4,050 kg (9,000 lbs), and Mess Cat hauled 5,400 kg (12,000 lbs) of fuel, provisions, explosives, and other gear. Lunch was at 1600, then more work, and dinner at 2000. Jackman did the cooking this time.

According to the evening radio contact with NAF McMurdo, the planes were scheduled to bring fuel for the Rolligon the next day. Jackman's VLT stint would be over. He would be evacuated to NAF McMurdo. The evening was devoted to writing last-minute letters to be given to the VX-6 flight crews, the last that would be mailed for three months or more—if our traverse was successful. Everyone was tired that night. Arnie's back was sore, and Tommy worried about the SnoCats and sleds being under such

Figure 4.7. Plateau Depot, VLT's supply cache at the top of the Skelton Glacier. In the foreground is the cache Edmund Hillary established in 1958 for Sir Vivian Fuchs' Commonwealth Transantarctic Expedition. Mess Cat is to the left, and Seismo with its Rolligon is in the center, beyond Detector.

Figure 4.8. Part of the supply cache laid for the VLT team at Plateau Depot.

Figure 4.9. Repacking the sleds at Plateau Depot.

Figure 4.10. Al, Lou, and Arnie, refueling a SnoCat from the Plateau Depot fuel drums.

Figure 4.11. Bill reloading sleds and 'Cats.

heavy loads. All were overloaded. As though to confirm Tommy's concerns, while moving Mess Cat to set up the radio antenna for the evening radio schedule, Mess Cat broke a steering tie-rod end. Tommy, with Jack and Frans' help, repaired it the next morning.

Monday, November 9. The temperature was −33 °C (−27.4 °F), clear, but the wind increased later in the day. Morning and early afternoon were devoted once more to packing and loading gear from the Plateau Depot onto the sleds and into the SnoCats (Fig. 4.11). Frans scouted the area for trash and debris, policing the area before the arrival of the aircraft, which, who

knows, might have a VIP or two aboard. Appropriately concerned, he was chided however by Tommy: "You'd eat out of a dirty bowl, but clean up the area for the VIPs!" The laughter from the crowd included Frans, who almost choked at breakfast.

At 1300 the first plane arrived (Fig. 4.12), an R4D with 400 gallons of fuel for Seismo's Rolligon. On board was Dr. Tom Jones (Fig. 4.13), Director of U.S. Antarctic Research Programs for the U.S. National Science Foundation (NSF). Frans was right—there was a VIP on board. Also on board was a Navy crew that went to work refueling the Rolligon (Fig. 4.14). Dr. Jones

Figure 4.12. The first refueling plane arrives.

retired to Mess Cat where, with the VLT team, he talked about the traverse, the contribution it would make to scientific understanding, and the potential risks involved. At 1530 a second R4D arrived, flown by Buzz Dryfoose. On board this second plane were Admiral Tyree, Commander of the U.S. Naval Support Force in Antarctica (Fig. 4.15), and Commander Bertoglio, the new Commanding Officer of NAF McMurdo. It was a gathering of dignitaries. The wind came up again, now with a vengeance, blowing snow beneath cold clear skies, as the party stood, talked, and shuffled to avoid the cold and wind, exchanging banter (Fig. 4.16). Soon the Rolligon was full, and our dignitaries reboarded the R4Ds (Figs. 4.17 and 4.18). As he departed, one of the officers said with a straight face, "I admire you—but I don't envy you!" We nodded our approval, and thanked him for the observation.

With JATO bottles ablaze, snow billowing from the ski tracks as the first plane departed (Fig. 4.19), Jackman left with Dr. Jones and other dignitaries. This would be the last any of us would ever see of him. He died soon after in the UK of unknown causes. Buzz's plane, the second, took off at 1700 in another blinding cloud of snow. Four large boxes had been left behind. The team opened them with delight—pastries, bread, and fresh good stuff. The team was very grateful for this support, radioing its gratitude at the evening's radio schedule with NAF McMurdo. It was no small thing to land two R4Ds at our location. Hard, rough sastrugi, high altitude, strong winds, and cold, VX-6 too took risks to make this enterprise successful. The VLT team continued.

Figure 4.13. Dr. Tom Jones, Director, U.S. Antarctic Research Programs for the National Science Foundation.

Figure 4.14. Navy crew from the first plane to arrive, refueling the Rolligon.

Figure 4.15. Rear Admiral David Tyree, Commander of the U.S. Naval Support Force in Antarctica.

Figure 4.16. Jack, Arnie, Al, and Admiral Tyree, conversing in the wind.

Figure 4.17. Lieutenant Earl D. (Buzz) Dryfoose with his R4D8, the second plane to land.

Figure 4.18. Frans thanking Buzz Dry-foose just before the R4D departure.

Figure 4.19. The first R4D buzzes Plateau Depot, wishing the VLT team God speed.

Chapter 5

Following Crary's trail

On Tuesday, November 10, the VLT team was still at Plateau Depot, at 2,134 m (7,000 ft.) elevation; the temperature was −40 °C (−40 °F); the skies were clear and sunny, and there was no wind. At breakfast, the VLT team discussed the previous day, the pleasant visit with the Navy crews and the well-wishing dignitaries. Now that the traverse team was well supplied, the conversation turned to more serious traverse matters. Ways were considered for departing earlier each morning. Frans and Jack suggested putting the water kettle in Bill's sleeping bag the night before, keeping it warm so Bill could heat it faster in the morning. Bill frowned, putting the kibosh on the "kettle in a sleeping bag" idea. He offered instead to get up a half hour earlier to start warming the kettle. Frans frowned. Cooking for the team, which at one point numbered ten hungry men, was done on the two-burner Coleman camping stove. Because the traverse would be traveling at altitudes that ranged from 2,134 to 2,744 m (7,000 to 9,000 ft.) above sea level, a pressure cooker was added to the cooking gear. Mess Cat was also equipped with a long table with folding legs, set up for meals, then taken down and stored on its edge against one wall of Mess Cat when traveling. Built-in benches on either side of Mess Cat gave everyone a place to sit. It was a crowded, but cozy arrangement.

Detector departed at 0930, stopping at an accumulation stake left by Crary's team. There they took measurements, and dug a 1-m pit to do stratigraphy. Finished by 1330, Arnie and Al, in Detector, moved on. At 1000, while repacking Mess Cat's sled, Tommy and Bill were the first to spy, unexpectedly, an Air Force C124 transport overhead. Circling several times, we thought to gain our attention, the plane disappeared over the horizon, then came back and circled again, dropping a parachute (Fig. 5.1). In the airdrop, we were pleased to find supplies: Tide, canned baked beans, matches, coffee, toilet paper, gloves, and camera film. The Tide was something of a mystery. There was no laundering on the VLT. Though unexpected, the drop was much appreciated, particularly because the plane had likely flown in from New Zealand.

Soon thereafter Mess Cat broke a tie-rod end and a right-rear spring, which Tommy quickly repaired. Arnie kept a notebook in which he recorded breakdowns and marked the traverse days.

The unofficial timekeeper of the traverse, Arnie would frequently remind the group that "There are only 'X' more days to go."

The unexpected equipment failures were not welcome so early in the traverse. And, of course, the team had no idea how well the SnoCats and sleds would stand up to the harsh conditions that lay ahead. Like the Rolligon, the other equipment used by the VLT team was an experiment, a risky one intended to evaluate its capability to survive harsh polar punishment. The traverse traveled until 1930 this day, made 22 km (14 miles), and saw no sign of crevasses. Mount Feather, off to the right, was a reminder that the VLT was now on the unexplored East Antarctic high plateau, that the traverse was now in Victoria Land! Our goal of completing our journey, always in doubt, reminded the team of Sir Ernest Shackleton's truly heroic if failed Imperial Trans-Antarctic Expedition of 1914–1917—a continent away.

On Wednesday, November 11, the wind was raw, and the temperature was −47 °C (−52.6 °F). Everyone was up early at 0800, and Detector, with Arnie, Al, and Lou, was under way by 0930. Claude, Jack, and Frans took off in Seismo, and Bill, Tommy, and Taylor followed in Mess Cat. Leaving the top of the Skelton Glacier and heading out onto the plateau, with fewer crevasses around, each vehicle traveled somewhat faster than when coming up the glacier. With fewer crevasses, each SnoCat was free to wander slightly from Detector's tracks, expressing, as it were, its driving independence. Now well off the glacier, at dinner that evening the conversation was more forgiving and relaxed. It was more relaxed that is until Frans and Taylor began a conversation about grid navigation. Seeming to be the only ones at the mess table who knew what grid navigation was, each asserted his own authority. And each had a different understanding of the process, shared firmly but collegially. Close quarters will do that to you. Al offered that he'd "give almost anything for some privacy—some mental and emotional privacy from such exchanges." Al's response was authoritative. Frans and Taylor cooled it. We all relaxed again.

The team was up at 0800 the next morning, November 12. Detector was on its way at 0900. Though the temperature was slightly warmer than the day before, −40 °C (−40 °F), there was the odd sensation that things were getting colder. While the

Figure 5.1. Air Force C124, making an airdrop to the VLT team just before their departure from Plateau Depot.

traverse had gained altitude, it was agreed that the deep soul and vastness of the East Antarctic high plateau had a chilling effect. Yet one could not help but appreciate its beauty. The surface was somewhat harder, preserving the year-old tracks of Crary's team. Detector therefore quickly found Crary's Station 73, and by 1600 had arrived at Crary's Station 84. Thirty-four accumulation stakes revealed an average snow accumulation of 5 cm (1.95 inches) for the year. Common for the high plateau, this was a low precipitation value compared to the continental average. Frans and Jack installed strain line stakes, stakes to be measured should another party find its way into Victoria Land years later. After dinner, Al and Arnie continued pit work they had started earlier, finishing ~2230. Claude melted snow samples that he had collected for isotope analysis. Arnie noted that Taylor had gone to bed. Ever since his experience with reduced visibility in blowing snow, Taylor tended to avoid such conditions. Four nights earlier, Taylor had moved to Seismo to sleep. Arnie, Al, and Lou slept in Detector, while Bill, Tommy, and Claude slept in Mess Cat. During dinner Al reflected on the evening when he and Arnie had been out until 0500 in the morning remeasuring strain lines at the bottom of the Skelton Glacier. It had been clear, calm, and very cold that night. They had seen some of the first crevasses close to the bluff. Al remembered: "That's when it hit me. I felt completely alone, isolated, and frightened. If the rest of the team had been along, we would have done the job with no difficulty, but as it was, the task was very hard for me to do." This was foreboding news. The traverse had traveled 27 km (17 miles), reaching the farthest point it would travel on Crary's trail, the VLT's first station 500. The next day the VLT team would strike a new trail north-northwest—this time into unexplored territory.

Taylor was the last in for breakfast and was silent throughout the meal. It was Friday, November 13. The team sat at the breakfast table longer than usual talking about the birds and the bees.

As though to change the subject, Jack advised the group that Friday the 13th was a lucky day for his father, and always had been for him. He expected good things this day. A few nodded their heads in agreement. The temperature was −38 °C (−36.4 °F); it was windy and sunny. Advised that there would be an airdrop, Frans guarded radio channel 6708 to see if the plane might make it this day. No early sign of it, so Detector left with Arnie, Al, and Lou at 0930. Seismo left with Jack, Claude, and Taylor, and Mess Cat left with Tommy, Bill, and Frans an hour later.

The VLT team struck off, then, to the northwest as the mountains diminished behind the sleds. The traverse made 37 km (23 miles) this day. Making good time, now free of the glacier, Detector used an entire tank of gas, and Seismo with its far heavier load reached the last stop on fumes. Fuel consumption became a major concern. Detector also had trouble with snow blowing into the carburetor. At dinner Jack suggested that if the weather deteriorated the following day, the traverse should nevertheless continue in order to travel farther into Victoria Land.

Digging the glaciological pit and spreading the seismic lines were difficult tasks in bad weather. Surface noise from blowing snow also compromised the seismic soundings, and made life in the pit uncomfortable. It was agreed that traveling was the better idea. Up the next morning at 0700, those in Detector left camp at 0900. Mess Cat had failed to start. Tommy, Frans, and Bill worked on it for two hours in strong wind and blowing snow, checking first the carburetor, then the fuel pump, and finally the fuel line, where Tommy found ice. The problem solved, Seismo and Mess Cat got under way at 1130. The delay meant only 24 km (15 miles) traveled, both SnoCats arriving at Station 502, the first major station established since leaving Crary's trail. Al and Arnie dug their pit 2 m (6.6 ft.) for stratigraphy, finishing by 2100, while Jack and Frans drilled a shot hole in the ice, laid out their geophone spread, and recorded reflection shots.

Now well into Victoria Land, the observational routine involved stopping every 48 km (30 miles) on average, where the team established a major station. These were the "station days" in contrast to the "travel days" agreed upon earlier. On station days, Al and Arnie dug a 2-m-deep snow pit for their glaciological observation. They observed and analyzed snow and ice densities, temperatures, and stratification. On station days, Frans and Jack carried out their seismic work, which involved manually drilling 16-m holes in which explosives were detonated. Reflection shots were made to determine the thickness of the ice, and refraction shots were made to determine both the depth to bedrock and the velocity of seismic signals in the ice. On travel days, Frans and Jack also made observations of Earth's gravity at each 5-km stop between station days. At such stops, a metal tripod, which was transported on Seismo's sled, was placed on the snow surface under Seismo's floor. In the floor was a hole that received the top of the tripod and onto which the La Coste gravity meter was then mounted. Careful manipulation of the dials enabled Jack and Frans to determine the strength of Earth's gravitation at that location. Meanwhile an altimeter reading was taken, and radio contact was made with Detector. A very substantial number of gravity observations would therefore be possible over the high plateau, depending upon how far the VLT would travel. These gravity data were later tied to the seismic data to produce true profiles of the subglacial topography and, thus, the thickness of the ice.

Because the team was tired as usual, cans of beer were thawed out for dinner. With new musical selections now in the air, "Calypso" by Harry Belafonte, and "Continental" were enjoyed for a change. They were not to Frans' taste, however. Describing them as "childish," everyone was secretly amused the next morning to hear him humming Harry's tunes! Another day and still no planes. Since leaving Plateau Depot, evening radio contacts with NAF McMurdo had been by continuous wave (CW)—Morse code. The radio frequencies on which the VLT team operated were recorded by Jack, each frequency depending upon the needs of the senders, receivers, or in case of emergency. These, then, are the radio frequencies that were available:

> Daily 2000 radio schedule with NAF McMurdo:
>   6836—CW and voice
> Alternate frequency for NAF McMurdo: 4738—CW and voice
> All times mainly emergency: 9001—CW
> All times ground to air: 6708—voice
> Scott Base and between vehicles: 5400—voice
> Ground to air, long range: 5641.5—voice
> Dumont D'Urville: 6365 send, 5500 receive
> Radio call sign of VLT: Generate 01

The standing radio schedule with NAF McMurdo each day was at 2000. The large radio, the ANGRC-19, failed to work, so it was relegated to a sled. The ANGRC-9 radio in Mess Cat, however, performed well with voice messaging until we reached the polar plateau. Until then, every evening, if not consumed in other duties, most of the team assembled in Mess Cat to hear the "polar news." Sometimes unintended messages were intercepted that related to the VLT, news not meant for the team. The VLT normally traveled until ~1900 or later each day. Mess Cat, in which the radio had been installed, was the last SnoCat into camp each day, making radio contact usually ~1930. Because CW became the primary mode for contact after the polar plateau was achieved, and because the SnoCats were gassed up by the rest of the team as soon as travel stopped, Frans and Bill were most often the only ones in Mess Cat at the scheduled radio time.

Sunday, November 15, was the first major station day on the Victoria Land Plateau. The VLT team position was 77° 28′S, 153° 06′E with the temperature at −35 °C (−31 °F). Although it was sunny with a light wind everyone was cold. It was cold inside the SnoCats. The rule was that no one was to use the personnel heaters in the vehicles, because they were gasoline operated and the fuel needed to be conserved for the gas-guzzling SnoCats. There had been one exception—when Frans thawed out his frozen finger. Breakfast that morning was leisurely, with Lou doing most of the talking. Everyone then went to work: Arnie and Al went back to work digging the pit they'd started the evening before. Jack and Frans drilled a 16-m (52-ft.) hole for a seismic shot, then laid out two geophone lines with twelve geophones in each line. After sounding warnings to the rest of the team, they detonated three seismic reflection shots, recording the seismic returns on the seismograph inside Seismo (Fig. 5.2). Lou and Taylor, in the meantime, were in Detector working up the sun shots Lou had made. Lou normally made eight to twelve sun shots each day at major stations. Relying on the best, they became the official location of the camp, to be sent to USARP as permanent records.

Every member of the VLT team, by the time the plateau was reached, had developed chill blains on his heels. Frostbite, usually on the right foot, revealed that the problem resided near the vehicles' accelerators. A small hole around the clutch and accelerator pedals was discovered in each of the SnoCats, the holes allowing frigid air around the driver's foot, which was exposed for hours during travel days. Red, purple, and itchy, the blains became a serious annoyance during the traverse and, according to a few, for some time after. The cold and wind, too, often made outside work difficult, sometimes slowing efforts to conduct mechanical repairs on the vehicles and sleds. This was especially true when it came to more delicate work that required removing one's gloves and mittens. At lunch Frans made it very clear to the group that Harry Belafonte's music was not sincere. Coming as something of a surprise, it was apparent that he had been agitated, and had been mulling over the music for some time. It precipitated a good discussion, although no one seemed to know, in a musical context, what "sincere" meant. Although an imaginative and creative bunch, when it came to Belafonte versus Mozart, Beethoven, Gustav Mahler, and Robert Schumann, Frans had the upper hand.

Figure 5.2. Jack, setting frequencies on the seismograph in Seismo.

A few hundred miles ahead, should the traverse get that far, the VLT team would change direction at Apex Depot, the location of the end point of the French Adélie Land Traverse (ALT) journey. The team would then head east onto the last leg of the journey (Fig. 1.6). At the present rate of travel the VLT was expected to reach Apex Depot around December 21. At 1800, Al and Arnie started another pit. Frans and Jack were under a tripod drilling a hole for another seismic shot—the third they'd made that day. Drilling, which was normally done by hand with a bit that allowed recovery of an ice core, was strenuous work. Jack and Frans had brought along a McCulloch gasoline-powered posthole digger, which they hoped would replace the manual drilling needed for seismic shot holes (Fig. 5.3). Repeated efforts to use the McCulloch posthole digger failed, not for design or mechanical reasons, but because the ice was so cold and dry. When drill rods were raised from the hole, the cold, dry, and pea-sized shards ran off the flights of the drill rod. Like hot dry sand, the ice shards poured back into the drill hole. What had seemed like a good idea had to be abandoned.

Frans and Jack returned to manual drilling (Fig. 5.4). Once completed, Jack and Frans detonated a Nitramon charge that generated seismic waves that reflected off the rock surface beneath the ice. An advantage of manual drilling, however, was that the ice core could be retrieved and given to Al and Arnie for glaciological analysis (Fig. 5.5). They were able to determine ice temperatures, stratigraphy, and densities at much greater depths than from the 2-m depth of their pits. Claude also made important use of the cores, taking samples from them for isotopic analysis. Such analyses enabled him to determine the chemistry of Earth's atmosphere and Antarctic weather of the deep past, of the Ice Ages, and of contemporary climatic change. From Claude's

Figure 5.3. Jack and Frans, using the gasoline-powered posthole drill to drill a hole for a seismic shot. This drill failed to do the job in the frigid ice and snow.

Figure 5.4. Jack, Frans, and Claude, manually drilling a hole for a seismic shot.

Figure 5.5. Jack and Frans, manually drilling a hole for a seismic shot. The drill bit and tube, behind Jack's right hand, collect the ice cores that Al, Arnie, and Claude analyzed.

work, the world would learn of the importance of greenhouse gases of the past and present, and of the nature and threat of global climatic change. It was from these and other cores, and from Claude's creative scientific work, that the science of our evolving atmosphere began, and for which he is internationally known and respected.[1]

---

[1]He has been awarded numerous medals including the Humboldt Prize in 1988 and France's Légion d'honneur in 2009. He is widely acclaimed for his papers in *Nature* (1987 and 1993) and *Science* (1993), as well as his books *Glaces de l'Antarctique: Une Mémoire, des Passions* (1991) and *L'Antarctique* (1997).

Once again, there was no airdrop. During an afternoon break, Al, Tommy, Arnie, and Bill drank hot chocolate in Mess Cat, talking about the trip and what they'd do when they got back home. They decided that a club should be formed for those who remained with the traverse for sixty or more days, or for those who had remained above 2,439 m (8,000 ft.) on the polar plateau for that period of time. Arnie suggested that the portable outhouse, *Explorers' Club*, be taken back to NAF McMurdo as a museum piece for posterity. It was agreed that this was an absolute must. It had become a historic item. Al planned to shave and put on a suit and tie when the team got

Figure 5.6. Al and Arnie, making a Ramsonde determination.

back to NAF McMurdo. We doubted, however, that he had a suit, much less a tie.

Bill had come down with an infection, which manifested with shivers, chills, and wooziness. Because of the numerous aircraft deliveries and airdrops, the group theorized that, since bacteria or viruses are sometimes released when unpacking boxes, especially in Mess Cat's "kitchen," this may have been the source of Bill's problem. In the meantime, Tommy thawed out a grease gun, with plans to grease Detector. Stymied, however, he'd been at this all day. Cold had frozen the grease to the consistency of putty. To make matters worse, the grease fittings on the 'Cat also

were frozen, preventing them from taking the grease. Relying on a blow torch, he managed to complete the project.

On Monday, November 16, the VLT left its station on the plateau at 1030. The temperature was a familiar −38 °C (−36.4 °F), and it was sunny with a light wind. Bill reported that his chills had gone away, but that he still did not feel well. Those in Detector took a Ramsonde reading every other station on that day (Fig. 5.6) to determine snow density. Mess Cat had trouble with transmission fluid, so dinner was not served until 2300.

November 17 brought an R4D to our position. The crew airdropped ten packages free fall (Fig. 5.7) with mail and spare

Figure 5.7. R4D, making a free-fall airdrop.

parts. Because Bill was still under the weather, Frans and Taylor offered to cook that evening. It was something of a special occasion, however, because this was Al's twenty-seventh birthday. No birthday cake—a can of biscuits accompanied by the "Happy Birthday" song would have to do!

The next day, Wednesday, November 18, it was again a familiar −38 °C (−36.4 °F), sunny and windy. The next fuel cache was a discouraging 256 km (160 miles) away. Fifty-five–gallon fuel drums on pallets had been dropped by parachute earlier by a U.S. Air Force C124 aircraft. It would be a challenge to locate the drop site somewhere on the vast plateau. No one had much to say at breakfast, recognizing the fuel problem and the challenge of finding the fuel cache. Taylor seemed upset, having also been disgruntled the past few days, and Bill continued to struggle with his infirmity. It was less than the usual promising beginning for the day. The traverse was under way by 0900, traveling 12 km (7.5 miles) when one of Seismo's pontoon axle bearings failed. Fortunately, the spare parts box contained the part. Tommy replaced the bearing, making this stop a major station (Fig. 5.8), rather than five miles farther, which had been the plan. A good decision, this allowed Tommy to also install a new throw-out bearing that had been needed on Mess Cat, while Frans and Jack, and Al and Arnie were able to begin their observations earlier.

Al and Arnie resumed digging their glaciological pit after a pause for hot chocolate and tea in Mess Cat. Both were exhausted, Al admitting he could lift only three shovelfuls of snow before needing to rest. Arnie stated that while he had no wish to leave the traverse, he wished the struggle was over. The temperature had been quite low with intense wind much of the time, making "pit" work and seismic work a challenge. In the afternoon it was cloudy and hazy, with near whiteout conditions. Tommy repaired the throw-out bearing on Mess Cat. Al and Arnie finished digging

their pit, and did density measurements on a 12-m ice core that Jack and Frans had retrieved. At the same time, Jack and Frans completed three more seismic reflection shots. The temperature was now −41 °C (−41.8 °F), and still windy. Although the demands on the staunch Tommy were increasing by the day, he admitted that evening that he might consider putting in a request for a job as a USARP mechanic, and returning to the ice as a civilian next year. There was little conversation or laughter at mealtime. The team was exhausted.

On Thursday, November 19, the temperature was −26 °C (−14.8 °F). No wind, but with whiteout conditions, it was nevertheless the warmest day in quite some time. At breakfast the group discussed whether to travel or do maintenance on the vehicles. Tommy noted that the tracks should be greased. Lou observed that because of the whiteout condition, we wouldn't be able to set a course because there was no sun for sun shots. Frans and Jack thought we should travel. Eventually the sun shone through, Tommy finished his work on Mess Cat's transmission, Al helped him grease the tracks, and the traverse got under way at 1330, making 21 km (13 miles) over an increasingly rough surface (Fig. 5.9).

At breakfast the next morning, Friday, November 20, Taylor, always one to "stir the pot," made some controversial remarks. Frans, following suit, characteristically tried to get an argument going. But by then most of the team members were wise to them, paying scant attention to their efforts. After breakfast Tommy made another attempt to grease the steering tie-rod ends. The grease gun once more froze. Frustrated, Tommy threw the grease gun and blow torch into the air. He paused, hands on his hips, then picked them up and successfully completed the task. The VLT team began its traverse at 0915, traveling at 3.2–4.8 kph (2–3 mph) over increasingly rough sastrugi. At 1145, Detector, monitoring radio frequency 5400, picked up a voice mes-

Figure 5.8. The snow surface was growing rougher by the day due to more and larger sastrugi.

Figure 5.9. Seismo, heading over worsening sastrugi with its sled and the Rolligon. On travel days, a trail flag was left at each station by Detector and picked up by Seismo.

sage, a call for help! A New Zealand field party was attempting unsuccessfully to radio Scott Base from somewhere out on the Ross Ice Shelf. Bill replied and learned from the urgent voice that the field party was radioing from the bottom of a deep crevasse! Their SnoCat, with three Kiwis in it, had broken through a snow bridge, falling 100 ft. to the crevasse bottom. One of the Kiwis had died in the fall, and two were injured. Located just east of the junction of Byrd Glacier and the Ross Ice Shelf, the Kiwis were some 240 km (150 miles) from the Skelton Inlet and 400 km (250 miles) from our position on the polar high plateau. Unable to raise Scott Base by radio, they requested help. Frans

then radioed NAF McMurdo on the international Mayday frequency, 121.5. The radio message was intercepted by Admiral Tyree's flight crew, who was in the air on a flight to the South Pole Station. Admiral Tyree then took command and ordered an NAF McMurdo rescue team to the accident site. McMurdo then launched one Otter and one helicopter to the scene. With a Navy doctor aboard and with the flight crews, the men were raised from the crevasse. Tom Couzens, a New Zealand army lieutenant, was dead. Jim Lowery, a New Zealand geologist, would lose both legs. Bernie Gunn, also a New Zealand geologist, had suffered a broken back but would survive.

Figure 5.10. The explosive Seismogel was used in large refraction shots for determining continental ice sheet characteristics at distances of up to 25 km. Because the Seismogel sometimes failed to detonate, Jack (left) and Frans (right) peeled off the thick cardboard covers of the Seismogel, which ensured that most of the explosive detonated.

At dinner that evening, the discussion was of course all about the Kiwis' accident. Tom Couzens, Jim Lowery, and Bernie Gunn were all good friends. And all were good polar explorers. Their plight brought back memories of the challenges we'd had on Skelton Glacier. Reawakened to the dangers of *The Ice,* the team realized that it could have suffered a similar fate, and might yet in the days and miles ahead.

Saturday, November 21, would be a major station day. Detector would go 19 km (12 miles) ahead, where Al and Arnie planned to dig another pit. Frans and Jack would drill an 8-m (26-ft.) hole at this location in preparation for a seismic refraction shot that they would make the next morning. This required that Seismo travel 16 km (10 miles) ahead to record the seismic energy from the detonation. Because the Seismogel had not detonated on a previous occasion, Frans and Jack judged that it was related to the low temperature at the bottom of the hole, and the thick cardboard covering on each stick of dynamite. Though involving risk, they decided that for seismic refraction shots to work, they would need to remove the thick cardboard covering from each stick of Seismogel before depositing it in the bottom of the drill hole (Fig. 5.10). That morning, the temperature was −28 °C (−18.4 °F); the skies were overcast, and there was no wind. Detector set out at 0900 with Arnie, Al,

and Lou, arriving 19 km (12 miles) ahead at 1500. Frans and Jack loaded the drill hole with 113 kg (250 lbs) of Seismogel. Jack drove Seismo ahead 16 km (10 miles), laid the geophone spread to detect and record the seismic energy, and then made radio contact with Frans. Frans had prepared the shot box and connected it to the wires that now extended from the Seismogel beneath the ice, up and out the ice-drilled hole. The wire was then connected to the shot box. At the countdown, Frans activated the shot box while Jack monitored the now live seismograph inside Seismo. But—the shot misfired. There was no explosion! Following a few expletives radioed between Jack and Frans, Jack then returned to camp, leaving the geophone spread in place. He and Frans then drilled a second hole adjacent to the first in an effort to intersect the Seismogel at depth. The plan now was to lower a smaller Nitramon charge into the Seismogel repository and, with the Nitramon, to detonate the whole. After the hole had been drilled and the Nitramon was in place, Jack drove back to the geophones. This time the shot was fired successfully (Fig. 5.11) at 2000, giving good results. It made a crater 7 m (23 ft.) across and 2 m (6.5 ft.) deep. Jack retrieved the geophones and cables, and returned to camp. Meanwhile Al and Arnie finished another pit and completed their data collections (Fig. 5.12).

Figure 5.11. Frans and Jack successfully make a seismic refraction shot.

Figure 5.12. Al and Arnie in the pit, determining firn temperatures, densities, and stratigraphy. Note that a canopy tarp was often used to cover the pit for photography, and when the weather deteriorated.

Chapter 6

Fuel cache in the desert

On Sunday, November 22, there were three in Mess Cat for breakfast. Frans, Tommy, and Bill enjoyed hotcakes and bacon. The others were at their distant stations doing seismic and glaciological work. It was hazy and overcast, with a 5 knot (5.75 mph) wind and a temperature of −29 °C (−20.2 °F). Bill shaved and brushed his teeth. Tommy, melting snow on an engine block, took a sponge bath and threw away his dirty clothes (Fig. 6.1). The VLT team used frequency 5400 when communicating by radio

Figure 6.1. Tommy, squeaky clean.

between 'Cats. At one point Frans, who was talking to Mess Cat, received an interruption. Scott Base came up and told him to "get off their frequency." It was Peter Yates, Scott Base's radio operator. Momentarily stunned, Frans objected. After a friendly interchange, Yates apologized, and the issue was resolved. That evening, to celebrate the successful refraction shot, all members of the team had a martini, listened to Radio New Zealand (always a pleasant interlude), and enjoyed Bill's dinner of ham mixed with corn, beans mixed with canned tomatoes, and other easy-to-forget ingredients. Cheered by the cocktail and Bill's warm food, the conversation moved quickly to the excitement of adventure, though Taylor and Lou were growing anxious and wanting the traverse to end. Hard to believe for the rest of us—we'd barely gotten into Victoria Land!

While both distance and fuel supply loomed as growing problems, the team was determined to travel as far as possible, and collect as much scientific data as circumstances allowed. Part of the problem was the heavy loads the SnoCats and sleds were carrying. Al suggested dropping fifteen barrels of fuel to lighten the loads, provided the VLT could reach the fuel cache. There would be ample fuel at the airdropped depot. Frans, Jack, and Arnie were uncertain, and the decision was made not to drop the fuel. The team believed it could locate the cache, and that abandoning the fuel was premature. Al agreed.

Tommy worked on Mess Cat's water pump, which was leaking antifreeze. Everyone else from Detector and Seismo congregated in Seismo to watch Jack receive a refraction shot that Frans set off from Mess Cat 16 km (10 miles) back. Jack had difficulty getting the timing motor on the recording device going, and Frans later reported that he could not hear Jack on the radio, so the shot was delayed. They ingeniously relayed their closely timed message through Scott Base, getting the shot successfully fired at 1400. After the refraction shot, Mess Cat set off at 1845 to join the others. The supper discussion was about how well or poorly team members were sleeping. Al and Arnie were waking up about every two hours. Al reported also that he dreamed more than usual. Tommy wasn't having any problems. Claude said he was sleeping lighter and waking up earlier than usual, and Bill reported the same. The team usually went to bed around

Figure 6.2. Claude, welcoming the return of the outhouse, Explorers' Club (hanging from Detector); Frans, observing disapprovingly.

2200–2230, sometimes as late as 2300. Some read before hitting the sack, and some spent time writing in their journals.

On Monday, November 23, the VLT was at 144° 47′E, 76°15′S. It was sunny, and the temperature −38 °C (−36.4 °F) with a light wind. At breakfast there was a spirited discussion about women and civilization. No conclusions were reached, but there was a wide range of opinions. Detector started out at 0915. Seismo and Mess Cat followed an hour later. The snow surface was rough, and the traverse made 3 mph at best. By 1500 the vehicles had traveled 19 km (12 miles) when the front tie rod on Detector came loose. Seismo and Mess Cat caught up to Detector at 1615 and by 1745, Tommy had it fixed. The traverse moved on for another 3.2 km (2 miles) before stopping for the day at Station 508 at 1900. Bill, looking for Explorers' Club, learned that Claude had left the outhouse at the last stop. Al, Arnie, and Lou unhooked Detector from its sled and went back to look for it. A treasured piece of gear, especially in a strong wind; Claude felt disgraced and was impressively apologetic. Al, Arnie, and Lou found it (Fig. 6.2). The day was saved (Fig. 6.3), and Claude was soon forgiven.

Urgency appeared in daily conversations because of diminishing fuel and equipment failures. Pleased and proud of their progress to date, the VLT team nevertheless was conscious of both problems. The traverse still had a long, long way to go. Finding the airdropped fuel cache was becoming increasingly important. The second problem dealt with the snow surface of Victoria Land—the hard, high sastrugi was punishing the vehicles relentlessly. Since leaving the Skelton Glacier, breakdowns were increasing daily. Spare parts were in dwindling supply. Inability to complete the traverse was a frequent concern.

Taylor confided in Bill that he felt ill and would ask for evacuation. Complaining of a cold, he thought it had infected his chest. Because he twice had pneumonia, Taylor believed

Figure 6.3. Al, coveting VLT team's prized possession.

he was at risk again. Bill advised Frans, who was upset by the news. Jack, Bill, and Frans met and talked it over, considering the seriousness of Taylor's condition and the danger a VX-6 crew would face in an attempted landing and evacuation. Frans was understandably reluctant to put others at risk for such an uncertain rescue. During the evening radio communication with NAF McMurdo, Frans reported that Taylor had asked to be evacuated. There were audible groans from Al, who asked Bill how bad Taylor was feeling. "Is he worried about getting out?" Bill answered, "I don't know." Uncomfortably, none of the team members was qualified to evaluate Taylor's condition. Dr. Brown, the VX-6 physician, asked Frans if Taylor's condition was serious enough for evacuation. Frans said he could not judge, and repeated Taylor's claims. After the radio schedule was concluded, Frans felt the strain of decision-making. Another radio conference was scheduled for 1200 the next day to determine if VX-6 could fly in to make the rescue.

The VLT was now a very long distance from NAF McMurdo at VLT Station 510, a straight line distance of 960 km (600 miles). VX-6 decided to make the attempt at rescue. A P2V flew to the VLT's position, and it was quickly apparent to the VLT team and the P2V crew that the heavy sastrugi would make a landing impossible. The P2V returned to NAF McMurdo, VX-6 deciding that they would attempt a helicopter rescue. Taylor worried that the helicopter might not make it far enough, asking about its range and whether it could make it back to NAF McMurdo. Taylor could take only the clothes he was wearing, his sleeping bag, and his camera because of the load limitations of the helicopter. The distance was beyond helicopter range, so the pilot reduced his crew to one assistant and unloaded all the unnecessary equipment. The P2V flew ahead dropping two fuel caches that would enable the helicopter to leap-frog the distance to VLT Station 510.

On Tuesday, November 24, the traverse traveled 16–19 km (10–12 miles). The helicopter, scheduled to be at our position at 1500, searched for its fuel caches with the P2V flying cover. Jack talked to the helicopter and P2V pilots as they were inbound, helping them locate the VLT's position. Both arrived at 2430 as the P2V flew overhead. The helicopter landed, piloted by Al Potter. The P2V was piloted by Wilson. Taylor boarded the helicopter (Fig. 6.4), and Lou and Bill were there to say goodbye. Lou carried Taylor's sleeping bag and loaded it onto the chopper. The others were some distance away. After the helicopter left, the P2V buzzed the camp on departure (Fig. 6.5), and the team got to bed at 0130. The VLT team went on without Taylor.

Wednesday, November 25, turned out to be one of the VLT's best travel days. Detector left at 0915, the others an hour later. The vehicles arrived at their final stop at 1930, having covered a distance of 35 km (22 miles). The surface had improved. Al and Arnie dug 2 m (6.6 ft.) of their pit by the time Seismo and Mess Cat arrived. At the evening radio schedule, Frans inquired about Taylor, and was told he was better and had sent his good wishes. Frans resolved not to ask for another such evacuation, no matter what the circumstances.

Thursday, November 26, was Thanksgiving Day. The team "slept in" until 0845. Jack and Bill "fixed things up" for a great Thanksgiving dinner. They kept everyone out of Mess Cat until everything was ready. Jack mixed martinis. Good cheer was followed by Bill's thawed beef steak, fruit cocktail, nuts, thawed peas, thawed corn, rice, bread, and cranberry sauce. After dinner the team enjoyed Arnie's New Zealand brandy and Taylor's abandoned cigars. By 1630 the temperature had risen to –20 °C (–4 °F), suitable to celebrate the holiday! After the evening meal the team left Mess Cat and went back to work, while Al played a tape from a girlfriend in New Zealand, which lasted about an hour and twenty minutes. Al seemed energized. Bill put the tape recorder on the roof of Mess Cat and played music while the team worked at its assignments, to the satisfaction of everyone, except Frans, who moaned that it was not classical. Not in a working mood because it was Thanksgiving, Arnie, and especially Al, found it difficult to work back in the pit. Taylor sent a message in the evening radio schedule saying that he was leaving for Christchurch and that he'd visit Bernie Gunn in the hospital. Taylor's thoughtfulness was appreciated.

On Friday, November 27, the VLT was at its Station 511, 75°30'S, 147°30'E. The temperature was –38 °C (–36.4 °F), sunny, with light winds. At 0900, Al talked to Charlie Wise via Scott Base on the radio. Charlie and his team were near the Goldie Glacier and expected to return to Scott Base on February 5. Al and Charlie discussed our mutual friend, Tom Couzens, who was killed in the New Zealand SnoCat crevasse accident. Detector left camp at 0915, and the others followed an hour later. The next day the traverse made good mileage, 35 km (22 miles) over a surface that was rough in parts and fair in others. The wind varied from 1 to 14 knots (1.15 to 16 mph).

Bill rode with Jack that day. To fill the time the team sometimes engaged in fantasy. This time the fantasy was, again, about food. Bill wondered what he and Jack would have for lunch in a more forgiving setting. Bill suggested martinis before lunch, swordfish, green salad, and coffee after. Jack preferred beginning with soup, chowder or oyster, then marinated herring. Not good for Bill—he didn't like it. Jack then suggested roast duck, and Bill added quickly "with plenty of dressing and strawberry shortcake, then apricot brandy and coffee." This discussion lasted for a couple of hours and made the miles pass quickly. At dinner the fantasies continued. Frans said he'd write all of us a letter. Tommy imagined, while driving Mess Cat, that he'd driven all the way from Davisville, Rhode Island, to Williamsburg, Virginia. There, he imagined, he had bought a black Nash Rambler[1], which he was now driving over sastrugi! These departures helped pass the time while traveling. The VLT was now ~85 km (53 miles) from the reported location of the next fuel cache that had been airdropped earlier. Claude, on a different note, related that when he asked, no one in Christchurch could tell him the number of people that would be on the traverse. When he asked who

---

[1]The first successful modern American compact car (*New Encyclopaedia Britannica*, 2005, p. 333).

Figure 6.4. Taylor, boarding the helicopter for evacuation to NAF McMurdo.

would be in charge, no one seemed to know. He also commented on his inability to manage the English language, preventing him from participating as much as he wished.

After supper, Jack, Tommy, Bill, Al, Claude, and Frans talked for two to three hours. Frans wondered about geologic exploration before the traverse. Jack had worked in South America for the Anaconda Company's Chile Exploration Company. Frans also had worked in the mining industry. This brought the conversation to working in deep mines, as both had done. All agreed the VLT was better. The conversation moved to Okinawa and Korea, where Frans had worked, as had Jack when he'd been

in the army. Al's experience in Greenland was especially of interest, given the present circumstances. Then Claude mentioned that he had not gotten a return ticket to France, hoping to spend time in Washington, D.C. Bill planned to visit the Alexander Turnbull Library in Wellington, New Zealand, to see what they might have in the way of original documents on polar exploration.

Sunday, November 29, was hazy in the morning and sunny in the afternoon with a 6 knot (6.9 mph) wind. The temperature was −32 °C (−25.6 °F). It was VLT Station 512 at 75°12.6′S, 146°38.5′E. Up at 0845, the team had breakfast, worked, then had lunch at 1500 and turned on the Armed Forces Radio Station

Figure 6.5. The P2V makes a departing pass before escorting the helicopter back to NAF McMurdo.

(AFRS) to listen to the Notre Dame–USC football game. Notre Dame won 16–6. Bill was happy because as a UCLA alumnus, it's good when anyone beats USC! Al and Arnie finished a 3-m (9.8-ft.) pit at 1730 and then did densities on the 16-m ice core Frans and Jack had recovered.

Claude helped Frans and Jack drill a hole for the seismic shot (Fig. 6.6). Tommy replaced a damaged water pump on Mess Cat. After lunch, Claude did his isotope sample work, and Tommy replaced a badly worn fan belt on Detector. Bill discarded one case of frozen meat, because it was moldy. The next case he opened was fine.

That evening the radio was set on frequency 11777, the *Family Corner Calling Antarctica* broadcast from New Zealand, which was on Sundays for fifteen minutes. Bill recorded the evening's dinner conversation for his "group research." Al and Arnie left Mess Cat, while Frans, Bill, Tommy, Jack, and Lou (who was washing dishes) discussed finding the next fuel depot. The U.S. Air Force had dropped fifty numbered flags perpendicular to the

Figure 6.6. Claude, preparing to help Jack and Frans drill a hole for a seismic shot.

VLT team's course. Frans and Lou noted that the plane would not have been able to determine its position within 16 km (10 miles), given the difficulty of positioning at high latitudes and, particularly from the air. Fifty drums of fuel had been parachuted. On circling, the aircraft crew reported that they were unable to see the drums or the flags on the surface. No one seemed particularly concerned, confident they'd find it. Good spirits prevailed. Claude was in especially good spirits, having collected excellent samples for isotopic analysis. Jack, Frans, and Bill played catch with an ice core; Bill gathered snow for water at breakfast, then went to bed.

On Monday, November 30, there was an 8–10 knot (9–12 mph) wind, and the temperature was −35 °C (−31 °F). Detector got away by 0845 and made 40 km (25 miles) by 1815 over a fair to poor surface. At 2200 the temperature warmed to −30 °C (−22 °F) with a 10–12 knot (11.5–14 mph) wind and a haze of ice crystals blowing 15 m (50 ft.) above the surface. Skies were clear. The sastrugi had grown quite large, although the traverse made 43 km (27 miles), leaving 42 km (26 miles) to Depot 300, the fuel cache.

On Tuesday, December 1, the temperature was a modest −30 °C (−22 °F) with a 10 knot (12 mph) wind. Mindful of our fuel and spare part challenges, the team reminded itself that it was just a few weeks until Christmas. That perked things up, and the traverse team made good mileage, 37 km (23 miles), that day. The sastrugi was now more moderate, and continued that way as far as the eye could see. Once on the trail, Frans worked on the radio. Nearing Depot 300, where the airdropped fuel was cached, the team looked forward to a break. Still Jack and Arnie were annoyed by some of the team's complaining. Lou had grown sullen. Claude, in contrast, seemed always happy. Bert Crary had remarked that the long traverses created stress. Each had his own technique for coping. Frans' technique was to repair whatever he could find. Jack wrote, completing his journal notes, and a book manuscript he said would make the traverse famous. Bill washed pans, Al wrote notes and moved boxes on the sleds, while Arnie frittered with the tools. Tommy talked about buying the shiny antique black Nash Rambler when he got home. That, he said, was the car for him. Many of the team's thoughts were about when the traverse was over. Lou planned to take his time, visiting Fiji on his return to the States. Al planned to go with a New Zealand girl and another couple to a beach near Auckland for a holiday. Frans said he didn't "give a damn for civilization," except to hear "good" music. Bill thought about making a tour of the Pacific, or going to Europe and picking up a VW Kombie wagon, or maybe going to Mexico for a couple of months. They talked and mused about hot showers, good food, sun on a beach, and pretty women. At the same time, there were signs of strain from both exhaustion and monotony.

Up at 0745 the next morning, a light wind and temperature of −38 °C (−36.4 °F) greeted the VLT team. After breakfast, Detector was on its way at 0900, with Seismo and Mess Cat getting under way at 1015. Concern about finding the fuel cache drop zone proved to be valid. The team could not find

Figure 6.7. Airdrop site at 300-mile depot, with four 55-gallon fuel drums per pallet. Sixteen pallets had been dropped equaling 3,200 gallons of gasoline.

it. It was decided that Detector, though its fuel was dwindling, would drive in widening circles around the camp in hope of extending the search farther, but without losing track of the camp. About 1030, Al, Arnie, and Lou spotted trail flags in the snow. Detector arrived at the first flag at 1115, then drove along a line of flags for several miles until fuel drums came into view (Fig. 6.7). It was 1430. The location of the 300-mile fuel depot was 74°34′S, 144°30′E. This was 11 km from the location of the drop zone that had been reported by the aircraft crew. With no GPS available to the C124 flight crew in those years, nor to the VLT team, the find was fortunate. Seismo and Mess Cat arrived at 1600.

The fuel cache consisted of 55-gallon drums, again four per pallet. Although the pallets had been dropped by parachute, the 'chutes did little to slow their descent. Many of the pallets were buried in the snow, with a few visible above the surface. The VLT team set quickly to work, detached Detector from its sled, and attached a length of cable to its rear hitch. After digging sufficient snow from on top of and around the pallets, the cable was connected to a pallet. Towing the pallets up and out of the snow enabled the team to disconnect the drums from the pallets. The drums, 135 kg (300 lbs) each, had to be wrestled onto the sleds.

Jack and Claude filled both Seismo and the Rolligon without extracting the drums from the snow (Fig. 6.8) by manually

Figure 6.8. Claude, filling the Rolligon with fuel pumped from drums buried in the snow.

pumping the fuel from the drums, leaving the drums in place. The rest of the team extracted pallets and fuel drums, loading the drums on the sleds. The fuel-loading operation was a taxing and time-consuming business. Everyone was exhausted by the time the work was done. The team, nevertheless, had gotten its reprieve. The traverse could continue. There were many miles yet to travel before finding the second such airdropped cache. But, the group's ruminations were pleasantly and surprisingly interrupted. They were hundreds of miles from the Southern Ocean when a Skua gull appeared, circling the camp. It should not have been there, given the distance to the coast. Coming out of the northwest, once it completed its inspection, it flew back in that direction.

Five kilometers before reaching the drop zone, Mess Cat had broken part of its universal joint, the part that clips the transfer case to the drive shaft. To keep going, Mess Cat was driven the last few kilometers with the drive shaft disconnected from the front pontoons. The choice was clear, either radio for another spare part airdrop, or go on with only the rear pontoons driving Mess Cat and its sled. Given the heavy load Mess Cat was towing, and the unrelenting sastrugi all the SnoCats were enduring, continuing on with Mess Cat in that condition would risk the loss of the vehicle and its load of provisions. It was decided to radio for another airdrop.

Frans advised the group that he was reluctant to ask for another airdrop, though most thought it was necessary. On the radio schedule that evening, Frans conceded and advised NAF McMurdo that a SnoCat had suffered another breakdown. He advised them further of our options, to continue risky travel or receive the needed part. The choice now was up to the USARP administrators. Frans and the team were off the hook, if once more at increased risk. The team was advised that a P2V would make the run; the spare part would be delivered. Understanding again the challenges of distance, breakdowns, and eventual additional crevasses, the team resolved to streamline the caravan. Gear not absolutely needed was offloaded, lightening the vehicles and sleds. Fuel consumption had averaged 2.3 gallons per mile, so the lighter loads would also save some fuel.

On Thursday, December 3, the team arose at 0830, ate breakfast, and then with the outside temperature at −37 °C (−34.6 °F) and a 5–8 knot (6–9 mph) wind, Seismo departed with Jack and Claude at 1030, traveling 13 km (8 miles), where they would lay out a geophone spread; then by radio contact with Frans, another refraction shot would be recorded. The rest of the team spent the morning unloading the sleds, pumping more fuel into the Rolligon, and loading fuel drums onto the sleds. Detector left at 1500, driving the 13 km (8 miles) to join Seismo. Now alone for three hours in Mess Cat, Tommy and Bill took advantage. They sipped hot buttered rum and talked—we all thought—about the team.

Those at the main camp slept until 0830, and were greeted with a 9 knot wind, a temperature of −32 °C (−25.6 °F), with clouds and haze. Bill served a very good breakfast—hotcakes. Jack had returned the previous evening with Seismo, while Al and Arnie remained at the 13 km (8 mile) stop, where they worked digging a pit all day, finishing around 1900. After breakfast, Seismo and Mess Cat left for Detector's position, while Tommy worked, unsuccessfully, at making a part out of a bulldog clip for the universal joint. Because of its universal joint problem, Mess Cat traveled with only one drive shaft for its rear pontoons, therefore becoming marooned atop high sastrugi. To free Mess Cat, its sled was detached, and it was towed off the sastrugi. It was 2310 when Tommy finished installing a new hydraulic pump on Seismo. Jack and Frans completed their refraction shot at 2430.

Chapter 7

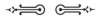

Seismo's discoveries — And disaster

The morning of Saturday, December 5, found most folks cheerful but exhausted. It was a quiet breakfast, except for Claude, who managed to keep his smile and good humor. The past few days had been grueling and strenuous, wrestling pallets and fuel drums, arduous manual drilling for a refraction shot, laborious digging of a deep pit, and making repairs to the vehicles. The team was tired, and understandably so. NAF McMurdo reported that a P2V from Wilkes Station would make the spare part drop that day. At 1800, a VX-6 R4D radioed saying that it was 96 km (60 miles) away, and headed for the team's position. The R4D arrived at 1845, airdropping spare parts, fan belts, beer, mail, and Swiss chocolate—which brought smiles to everyone.

On Sunday, December 6, before the SnoCats departed, two Skua gulls once more flew around the camp and then departed. It was hazy with blowing ice crystals and −30 °C (−22 °F). By noon the wind had picked up to 22 knots (25 mph). Seismo and Mess Cat departed at 1010 when, having traveled 12 m (40 ft.), Seismo's rear fifth wheel broke (Fig. 7.1). Tommy, Jack, and Claude got on it immediately, replacing Seismo's fifth wheel, while Frans worked on installing the ANGRC-9 radio in Mess Cat. Bill put on water for tea, coffee, and hot chocolate. Freezing was a constant risk for team members, who often worked without gloves, if only for brief seconds. Arnie's nose was the evidence—he'd been frostbitten so often the flesh turned white, and he suffered from some pain. Hours later, Seismo was repaired. Back inside Mess Cat after working outside in the cold, one's mind was somewhat numb with the well-known *fifty-foot-stare-in-a-ten-foot-room*, until blood refilled one's veins.

It is worth noting that manners and civility were maintained, notwithstanding the occasional grouchiness. "Thank you" for passing food was common. "Please" and "excuse me" were liberally used. Respect was maintained for contrary views and principles, and for one's beliefs—so was respect for each one's living space—for elbow room sitting at breakfast, lunch, and dinner, where space was tight. Entering Mess Cat was always preceded by a knock on Mess Cat's door. Claude was great at sympathetic understanding. He commonly inquired of Tommy how his work was going, knowing the tough job he had, especially following a day of difficult repairs. And Claude

asked about Tommy's plans when the traverse was over. This always cheered Tommy up.

At 1450, Seismo moved up to test the new fifth wheel. Tommy, again, had done the job. It functioned well, although equipment failures continued. At 1915, a half mile from the last station, Seismo broke its left rear spring. It snapped in two. The VLT team made camp, and Tommy stepped up again, repairing Seismo's spring. The team had traveled 17 km (10.5 miles), which meant extra driving the next day to make up the shortfall. Arnie left during dinner to listen to the *Family Corner Calling Antarctica* radio broadcast. It was a good way for him to get the news from home and usually cheered him up.

Frans often came early into Mess Cat to light the stove and start the engine, for the comfort of Bill, Claude, and Tommy, who appreciated his efforts. To put things in perspective, Claude recounted his experience at Charcot station, the year before: "Inside the hut, I would sometimes feel depressed. Three of us lived and worked for twelve months in a space that was 2 meters [6.5 ft.] high, 4 meters [13 ft.] wide, and 6 meters [19.6 ft.] long. A heavy curtain hung to provide some privacy. Sleeping was difficult, interrupted often by the noise of my fellows working. When I went outside to read my instruments, I would sometimes lie on my back and gaze up at the stars. I then felt good, until I went back in the hut."

A long period of polar exploration takes, it seems, a toll. But well-meaning jabs and good humor were more the order of the VLT team's day. When departing Mess Cat after meals, the small door was a tight fit, sometimes with excess traffic coming through. Taylor had handled it well: "Lady with a baby coming through!" So, by-and-large, civility prevailed, and each team member, without fail, met his responsibilities.

The greatest elevation reached since leaving the head of the Skelton Glacier was 2,804 m (9,200 ft.). The traverse had been traveling over very rough sastrugi. Bill measured some to be 0.9–1.2 m (3.0–4.0 ft.) high, and often hard as rocks. In spite of the steel tracks, the vehicles, more frequently than not, left little evidence that they'd been there. The direction of the constant katabatic wind was always south to north and so also was the sastrugi. The direction of travel was mainly from east to west, almost perpendicular to the sastrugi. The result was that the SnoCats took

Figure 7.1. Tommy, working under Seismo, replacing the fifth wheel.

a beating, and it slowed the rate of travel. Cracks had developed early in the structure and windshields of the SnoCats, sometimes opening and closing as the vehicles rode over the sastrugi. And, while a comfortable ride was out of the question, team members often napped amid the crashing and rolling. Although the sastrugi was unrelenting, it was also beautiful (Fig. 7.2). Artistic in design and glistening in the sunlight, it reminded one of nature's grace and creativity—it was good!

On Monday, December 7, the temperature was −30 °C (−22 °F) with a 10 knot (12 mph) wind. Someone noted at breakfast that it would be great to be lying on a beach in Hawaii. There was no disagreement as the team hurried to their stations, and hit the trail. The VLT team made 21 km (13 miles) over a very rough surface, stopping at 1430 to put in Station 519. Al and Arnie dug 2 m (7 ft.) of their pit by 1700, and had made density determinations from a 7-m (23-ft.) ice core, while Jack, Frans, and Claude had drilled a Nitramon reflection hole. Claude's help with drilling was always welcomed by Jack and Frans because manual drilling was extremely difficult. When finished, they were always exhausted, although pride prevented them from saying so. Dr. John Cook of crevasse detector fame once wrote that it is almost impossible for four healthy men to hand drill over 19 m (62 ft.) at this altitude and temperature. The seismic holes, normally drilled by two on the high plateau, were 16 m (52 ft.) deep. Although

Figure 7.2. Sastrugi on the high plateau—threatening yet beautiful. "There is no end to Nature's extravagant creations" (Weihaupt, 1979).

the temperature had warmed to −18 °C (−0.4 °F), the wind had increased to 25 knots (29 mph), making work all the more difficult. When it was time for lunch, Bill thawed beer in Mess Cat's engine compartment. With little enthusiasm for beer because of their exhaustion, Jack, Frans, Claude, Al, and Arnie did not consume much, to Bill's disappointment.

The seismic drilling crew and the glaciological pit digging crew returned to their work when lunch was done. When the seismic hole was completed and the glaciological pit had been dug, the crews caught their breaths before dinner, and then assembled in Mess Cat to eat and again share their ruminations. Whiteouts were a common topic of conversation. They had been abundant back on the trail (Fig. 7.3). Tommy observed that Larry Green, a Navy colleague at NAF McMurdo, described falling down when standing still in a whiteout, because he was disoriented. Arnie described a similar experience that had happened while he was on a pair of skis. Tommy offered that he'd once felt the sense of flying while driving onto the airstrip at McMurdo in a whiteout. The difficulty of determining size and distance was something that all had experienced. Al described seeing an oil drum at some distance near White Island left by the British Commonwealth Antarctic Expedition. On close examination it revealed itself to be a five-inch ration box. And, he'd had a similar experience in Greenland when he'd spotted a Quonset hut that, later, resolved itself into an oil drum—again in a whiteout. Someone else told of an article by Sir Raymond Priestley in which his colleagues had seen a driver and a dog team semaphoring at some distance, until the truth emerged. It was a tribe of penguins, waddling away. And Captain Robert Falcon Scott is said to have once thought he saw a dog team that turned out to be a piece of film wiggling in the breeze. Whiteouts can be unsettling, and, of course, a number of explorers have stepped into whiteouts, never to return.

Polar stories and adventures are abundant, of course, as are mirages and misconceptions. The previous day, Seismo and Detector had gone ahead a half mile for Frans to read the magnetometer. First setting up some distance from the vehicles to avoid magnetic interference, Frans paused, then came running back to Seismo. "An airplane! An airplane's nearby, near the camp! Can you hear it?" Jack paused, saying he too could hear it, but then came to realize it was not a plane at all. It was Mess Cat's engine purring; they had come to join the rest of the team at the station. Such stories are abundant, the products of adventurous minds and creative imaginations. Some self-proclaimed adventurers will give a different slant but, this is the way it really is.

Still at dinner that night, Al explained that while pit digging it occurred to him that the team was now experienced for another adventure. One such adventure could involve returning to the region of the Tucker Glacier where a two-year project of measuring the glacier's movement, including seismic work, would be an important scientific contribution. The beauty of the idea was that, if the VLT team could make it to the vicinity of the Tucker Glacier at the end of the traverse, the SnoCats could be recoverable for work on the Tucker. The following summer the SnoCats, then at the bottom of the glacier, could be driven up-glacier to complete the work of re-measuring to determine accumulation and movement on the glacier. The idea received considerable attention. The question arose, of course, about crevasses on the Tucker Glacier. No other teams had visited it except for Al's aerial reconnaissance. Little was known about the hazards the team might face. After dinner, Al, Arnie, Jack, Claude, Bill, and Tommy explored the idea until late in the night. A National Science Foundation grant would be needed. That slowed the conversation somewhat because of the need to prepare a grant proposal, and the administration it entailed. Serious consideration of such an undertaking was evidence that the challenges faced by the VLT team did not stem the team's taste for further adventure.

On Tuesday, December 8, there was light snow later in the day, and a warmer temperature of −16 °C (+3.2 °F) and a 15 knot (17 mph) wind settled in. Tommy took another sponge bath. At lunch, again with more creative talk, the conversation turned to how the team might lay out an airstrip, should the need arise. Leveling the sastrugi was the first requirement. Not an easy task, Al suggested dragging crevasse detector booms across the rough sastrugi. Arnie suggested lashing fuel drums to the booms to give them weight. Removing the skis from a sled and dragging it was also suggested, but Tommy vetoed taking a sled apart. No dearth of imagination, muscles and minds still were active. After dinner, the team listened to Frans' classical music; this time it was Mahler. It was 2200 as again a Skua gull scouted 'round the camp. In the past few days several Skuas circled before flying off toward the coast. Al and Arnie finished a 3-m (9.8-ft.) pit by 2200. Frans and Jack drilled and completed three seismic shots.

Wednesday, December 9, was a warm −25 °C (−13 °F) and sunny day. But ahead, over the horizon, clouds threatened an approaching storm. The weather grew changeable, and soon the traverse was in a whiteout, with the SnoCats' tracks impossible to see. Detector became marooned atop a wave of large sastrugi. The visibility was so poor that the men stumbled on the sastrugi. In spite of the whiteout and ubiquitous rough sastrugi, the traverse team made 34 km (21 miles). Tommy installed high-altitude jets in the carburetors of all the 'Cats, giving them more power and greater fuel efficiency. Following Detector's lead, Seismo became marooned also atop sastrugi, breaking the crossbar of the front runner on its sled. Upon stopping at 1500, Tommy discovered that the bearing on the left-rear pontoon axle extension of Mess Cat was badly damaged. He quickly replaced the bearing, but had no end part, making it uncertain that it would survive for very long. After a long day of bouncing over rough sastrugi, refueling the 'Cats got under way. Lou grumbled at Jack, "Aren't you going to help me refuel?" Jack replied, "I am, but you never help Frans and me drill our seismic holes." Greatly offended, Lou said, "The hell I don't, I helped once." Jack winced, and Lou's grouchy talk subsided.

On December 10, it was warm enough to drive with the windows and roof hatches open on the 'Cats. With no wind, the temperature was a balmy −17 °C (+1.4 °F). Clear overhead, Detector got under way at 0900, followed by Seismo and Mess Cat. An

Figure 7.3. Seismo, traveling in a whiteout. Neither sky nor horizon are discernible.

hour later, Seismo's left-rear pontoon axle extension bearing fell apart. It took 25 minutes for Tommy to repair it, with help from Jack, Claude, and Bill. This left the traverse with only one more bearing. Tommy figured at least five more would be needed. At 1425, a Skua made another pass. The VLT team made 34 km (21 miles) that day over a very rough surface. Detector stopped at 1630 when Seismo reported it was having its pontoon bearing replaced. Al and Arnie started on Station 521 and dug 2 m (6.6 ft.) of their pit by 1800 when Seismo and Mess Cat pulled up. After dinner, everyone went outside to enjoy the warmth. Claude and Jack took out a small can of pecan roll to use as a football. Except for Frans and Arnie, everyone played the game—passing, running, and throwing the can around. Tackling became part of the game. A good change of pace, it was also a good workout. Frans took pictures as Arnie stood by amused. The "game" went on for half an hour before the players headed for their sleeping bags.

The following day, Friday, December 11, the weather remained clear and sunny, but the warm temperatures were gone. It was −31 °C (−23.8 °F). This was a major station day; so there was no travel. At 1500, a Skua again appeared. The traverse team was confident this meant they were getting closer to the Southern Ocean. Al and Arnie finished their pit at 1800 as the temperature warmed up to −18 °C (−4.0 °F), with no wind, another sign the team was probably nearing the ocean. Al put his mattresses on top of Detector for sunny comfort and to air it out (Fig. 7.4). He and Bill sat on them for about an hour, soaking up the polar sun.

This fair weather made the work much easier, and everyone was in a good mood. Arnie, Tommy, Al, Claude, Lou, and Bill took pictures. Frans and Jack were busy making seismic shots. The best reflection shot revealed an ice thickness of 3,217 m (10,552 ft.), a very substantial continental ice sheet thickness much greater than encountered elsewhere on the high plateau.

Figure 7.4. Al and Bill, on top of Detector Cat, airing out Al's mattresses.

The station, at an elevation of 2,494 m (8,230 ft.), put bedrock 723 m (2,386 ft.) below sea level. Jack and Frans puzzled over this for the rest of the day, checking their instruments and calculations, all of which seemed right. They then brought out their previous seismic records for comparison, checked again the records and the data, and concluded that the Victoria Land Traverse had made a major discovery. Further examination of the data revealed that they had made not one, but two major discoveries. The collective records profiled the rock beneath the ice, a vast lowland between the head of the Skelton Glacier and the camp's present position. It was a subglacial basin larger than any yet known in East Antarctica. That was the first major discovery (Appendix A). The second was the unusual and much greater thickness of the continental ice sheet locally, in the vicinity of the camp. An apparent round, vast subglacial lowland lay unseen hundreds of meters beneath the snow surface. The subglacial topography beneath the camp was strange. It was complex. Not only that, the paleoclimatic discoveries Claude would make from his isotopic analyses, and Al and Arnie's ice stratigraphic profiling of Antarctica's recent atmospheric past, would one day add to the discoveries of the VLT. Jack and Frans were ecstatic, if somewhat muted. They shared their discoveries at breakfast with the team. All rejoiced in the news—and in Bill's "good" cooking!

At the end of the day Arnie listened to Scott Base communicating by radio with one of its New Zealand field parties. It was also learned from the evening radio schedule with NAF McMurdo that the Navy VX-6 Constellation would arrive there from New Zealand. Frans took the opportunity to advise them that the traverse needed spare parts, including bearings for the pontoons. The surface over which the VLT was now traveling was unusually rough, although Detector had gotten into fourth gear for several miles the day before. Al changed his underwear and pants, and Frans quickly set the abandoned clothes on fire. Claude cut Tommy's hair (Fig. 7.5). At 2300, the temperature was −25 °C (−13 °F) with no wind. It was quite comfortable.

Saturday, December 12, was another nice day: −31 °C (−23.8 °F), no wind, and sunny. Al and Arnie had not slept well the previous night. Al dreamed that, with some friends, he was rolling down a steep hill into Detroit when the truck he was driving ran away. Then one of the passengers went insane. The team had all sorts of fun with that story! For the past several weeks Frans had been dreaming of Indochina, a place of which he was quite fond. At breakfast, Lou asked for jam to be passed. Then came the chorus—"No!" Confused and surprised, Lou finally realized his folly. Sometimes a bit too demanding, Lou often put himself at risk of being confronted because of his uncongeniality. Then Lou laughed, recognizing it as good humor. The traverse made 38.6 km (24 miles) that day. The SnoCats took a severe beating, although there were no equipment failures.

On Sunday, December 13, there was no wind, and the temperature was −33 °C (−27.4 °F). Detector left camp at ~0830 and was about half an hour away when its front tie-rod end broke. Seismo and Mess Cat joined Detector, and Tommy, Al, and Jack fixed the tie-rod end. The traverse continued until 1300 when Seismo, trying to surmount some very large sastrugi, became suspended. Seismo was detached from its sled, and then was pulled free by Mess Cat. At 1730, Detector called Seismo to say that they'd broken the bracket that holds the fifth wheel to the chassis of the vehicle. On the way to assist Detector, Seismo and Mess Cat came across the draw bar of Detector's sled. One of the ends had broken, and the entire unit had fallen onto the snow, unbeknownst to Detector. Tommy and Frans attempted to weld the fifth-wheel bracket using bailing wire as a welding rod and electric current from the two remaining SnoCats' batteries, with their engines roaring. It didn't work. They then tried nails as welding rods, which was also unsuccessful. After further inspection, it was discovered that, in addition to the fifth-wheel problem, the braces on the chassis and the braces across the chassis were cracked at their welds. A broken track roller on the outside front-right pontoon of Mess Cat was next discovered. The team set to work helping Tommy. The repairs took four hours. The team got to their sleeping bags at 2300.

The next morning, December 14, was hazy with clouds and whiteout conditions that cleared by 1000. The small banana sled was disconnected from Detector and attached to Mess Cat because Detector could no longer pull more than absolutely necessary with its cracked frame. The team entered Mess Cat at 0745 for a bowl of oatmeal and a cup of hot chocolate. Detector soon departed. Jack checked Seismo and its sled, while Tommy and Bill did the same with Mess Cat and its sled. It was decided that they could hit the trail. In Seismo the altimeter and magnetometer were read before leaving, and Jack was busy copying seismic and gravity data. The ANGRC-9 radio in Seismo was turned on, and Detector radioed that it had arrived safely at its first stop. Seismo started out, followed by Mess Cat, as another day of driving over very rough sastrugi began. The traverse team made 8 km (12 miles) over the extremely rough surface, stopping for the day at 1500. Al and Arnie began digging their pit, getting 2 m (6.6 ft.) done by 1900, and Frans and Jack prepared for the next day's seismic observations.

The morning of December 15 was cloudy with a light wind and −28 °C (−18.4 °F). Bill shaved. Jack considered taking a sponge bath using snow melted in the engine housing, suggesting it also for the rest of the team. But no one else seemed interested. Claude, Jack, and Bill brushed their teeth on a regular basis. Claude also shaved. Al and Arnie, up at 0830, worked all day and finally completed their glaciological pit that evening at 1800. Frans and Jack drilled a hole for the seismic detonation and made another successful reflection shot by late afternoon. They found the ice thickness at this station to be 3,129 m (10,265 ft.), an anomalous thickness that Frans and Jack continued to ponder. By 1715 the temperature was −24 °C (−11.2 °F). On the evening's radio schedule, Frans asked NAF McMurdo for a welding rod. In the meantime, Tommy put a bolt through the fifth-wheel bracket on Detector, but it was questionable that it would hold. Tommy thought the crack came from a hole burned in the frame at the factory when the brace was fabricated. Lou calculated that it was

Figure 7.5. Claude, with Tommy's shoulders thoughtfully protected, cut Tommy's hair. Jack's hair was next on this December 11, which was Jack's brother Dave's birthday.

~144 km (90 miles) to French Station B-61, the VLT's Station 531, also called Apex Depot.

It was overcast the next morning, December 16; but by 1000, the sky had cleared. There was a 6–10 knot (7–12 mph) wind and a temperature of −27 °C (−16.6 °F). Detector left camp at 0900; Seismo and Mess Cat left at 1000. Four hours later it was discovered that a food box had fallen off the banana sled! Claude, in Mess Cat, traveled back a half mile to retrieve it, while Seismo continued on. At 1530, Mess Cat broke the right-rear tie-rod end. Having no suitable radio, Mess Cat was unable to contact Seismo. Tommy had only a left-hand–threaded tie-rod end to fit the right-hand–threaded tie rod. That meant an awkward repair of cross-threading and clamping the tie-rod end in place. Then, as Seismo moved out, its two front sled runners broke and were detached from its sled.

Two cross-chains, connecting the front sled runners to the rear runners, pulled the rear sled runners to the front of the sled, dropping the sled bed onto the snow (Fig. 7.6). The sled and its runners were separated. In addition to determining the extent of damage, it would be necessary to offload the entire sled, including the fuel drums, to repair the runners and the bed. The sastrugi surface had been brutal (Fig. 7.7), pounding, twisting, and wrenching both SnoCats and sleds. Mess Cat's windshield cracks had widened.

Seismo's accident was a major event. Only halfway through the traverse, it became apparent that SnoCats and sleds might not survive the journey. It was now uncertain if the team's goal would be achieved. The French traverse end point still lay a considerable distance ahead, and if that were reached, the traverse had yet to travel eastward of that station nearly a thousand miles to the Transantarctic Mountains. Jack, Arnie, and Tommy began the task of offloading Seismo's sled (Fig. 7.8). The task took two

Figure 7.6. The front and rear runners of Seismo's sled were pulled from under the bed of the sled. Seismo, not knowing and continuing on, pulled the rear runners ahead, rotating the entire sled, the rear now facing Seismo.

Figure 7.7. The sastrugi had grown in size and intensity as the VLT team ventured farther into the high plateau. Nature's creativity is evident in both the grace and chaos with which its brush had painted.

hours, revealing that most of the essential sled parts were intact, including the bed, runners, and cross-chains that articulated the sled when it turned. Once more the VLT was lucky. The accident could well have been the start of the traverse's demise. The offloading was done with care, organizing the sled load into categories to facilitate reloading as well as the order in which the sled contents would be used.

The challenge now was to determine how best to put the sled together. Because the bed of the sled had been rotated by Seismo after the break had occurred, it was rotated back again by Tommy driving Mess Cat. Jack and Arnie manned the chains and runners to keep them clear of damage and to orient them properly. The runners and their connectors to the chains and sled needed repairs. The steel runner front bar was attached to the fronts of both runners; the sled horizontal wooden front member needed to be properly reconnected to the sled and then to the wooden front member above the runners. The entire effort was undertaken with some care to avoid another such happening. Eventually Seismo's reconstructed sled was attached again to Seismo's Rolligon, and the full rig was put back together.

Figure 7.8. Arnie, Jack, and Tommy, working on a sled runner, with the sled "jacked up" by boxes to allow the reinsertion of the orange runner bar.

Next came the reloading, which was a three-hour operation this time. Jack, Arnie, and Tommy again took on the task. Fuel drums first, up front on the sled in their usual location close enough to Seismo to allow hand pumping from the drum to the vehicle's tank. Then came the multitude of boxes, provisions, spare parts, and, at the rear, seismic explosives well removed from the fuel. Next came the careful checking of the load to assure that there would be no unnecessary shifting of the cargo as Seismo rolled over the high sastrugi. That evening we talked about equipment failures, the team's experience to date, and the challenges that lay ahead. Lou had determined that B-61 was not far away. The important scientific connection with the ALT, the French traverse of the year before, would be the turning point at which the traverse would head east for the Transantarctic Mountains. Locating B-61 was essential to the traverse's scientific success. At 2330, the temperature was −28 °C (−18.4 °F).

The sky was clear the next morning, Thursday, December 17, with clouds in the distance, a 5–8 knot (6–9 mph) wind, and a temperature of −30 °C (−22 °F). Detector returned from reconnoitering the area, joining Seismo and Mess Cat, arriving at 1000. During breakfast, everyone was focused on the breakdowns. There was concern about how long the 'Cats and sleds would last, considering the beating they were taking. It was suggested that a SnoCat or two might need to be abandoned. No one seemed eager to leave the breakfast table, and the men sat and talked much longer than usual, exploring further the situation. Some consideration was given to attempting to reach Dumont d'Urville, the French station on the Southern Ocean. There it might be possible to construct an airstrip for evacuation. If conditions were right, a ski-equipped VX-6 plane might make it or, if not, a helicopter from an icebreaker that could make it through the sea ice to the coast. This was the first time any serious mention had been made of evacuation. We also considered the possibility of walking 300 miles oversnow from B-61 to Dumont d'Urville Station. Claude thought that was a grand idea.

Chapter 8

Apex Depot

On December 17, there was some consternation at the camp. Mess Cat's fifth wheel was the next to break down. Tommy, Claude, and Bill replaced it before lunch, tilting the vehicle and tipping pans and dishes inside Mess Cat. A full kettle of water from the Coleman stove tumbled to the floor, which Bill swabbed down. Before resuming the traverse, Tommy discovered that the cross bar for the front of the rear runners on Mess Cat's sled had dropped off and been lost. Jack, Frans, and Al jury-rigged the sled by running a cable through a timber, a wooden boom from the crevasse detector. At 1630, the temperature was −23 °C (−9.4 °F), with a biting 10–12 knot (12–14 mph) wind, clear skies, and sunshine. Radio America reported that this day was the fifty-sixth anniversary of man's first powered flight[1]. On the evening radio schedule, NAF McMurdo reported the VX-6 Lockheed Constellation had sighted a Russian traverse 280 km (175 miles) south of Vostok Station in three Russian SnoCats, with seven scientists aboard.

On Friday, December 18, the temperature was −30 °C (−22 °F). The sastrugi was less punishing that day. The SnoCats skirted a bowl-shaped depression, then came upon a long trough in the surface of the ice that ran east-west and roughly parallel to our track for a good five miles. Fifty (164 ft.) to 100 m (328 ft.) deep, the trough was uncommonly deep for an ice surface feature. Anomalous ice terrain, it was reminiscent of the seismic soundings Jack and Frans had made that revealed the vast subglacial lowland. The unusual ice surface constituted another VLT team discovery, a glaciological anomaly.

Preventative maintenance was done on Detector's sled. A worn chain link and a cotter pin for one of the sled skis were replaced. Al radioed Christmas greetings to his family, and to Neil Hamilton and his family in Christchurch. Tommy washed his feet that evening. Claude said he'd had a *very* good dream the previous night, but woke up disappointed. We made 36 km (22.5 miles) that day. On the evening radio schedule with NAF McMurdo, the team learned that a P2V would make an airdrop on December 23, and the Super Constellation would arrive at NAF McMurdo from New Zealand sometime tomorrow. Lou was in a cranky mood again—Al and Arnie picking on him as usual—with a few jabs from the rest.

On Saturday, December 19, there was a light breeze, and the temperature remained the same. Breakfast finished, Detector got under way at 0900, with Seismo and Mess Cat following an hour later. Around 1130 as Mess Cat was traveling over high sastrugi, it stripped several teeth from the beveled gear in the rear differential, leaving parts of the teeth lying in the bottom of the housing. At noon radio contact with Detector, they were advised of the breakdown and that it would take five hours to fix. Seismo returned at noon. Mess Cat was repaired by 1530, then drove four miles to join Seismo and Detector where Al and Arnie were digging their pit, at Station 527. By evening they'd dug 2 m (6.6 ft.) and taken photos (Fig. 8.1). By 1900, they'd finished their stratigraphy.

Jack, Frans, and Claude drilled a shot hole to 17 m (56 ft.) in three hours. They were exhausted, but set out the geophones and made three seismic shots, which yielded good returns. Revealing the thickness of the ice, the seismic data effectively depicted the subglacial topography, confirming the presence of a substantial basin. Eventually it would be shown that the basin is 510 km in diameter, representing a major topographic anomaly. The immediate question was what the feature represented. In the late afternoon and evening, reflecting on the seismic discoveries of this basin and the vast interior lowland, Jack and Frans puzzled over their discoveries. Remembering too the chaotic ice surface overlying the subglacial topographic anomaly, they could only conclude that the two were connected. While examining their geophysical data, it became clear that the gravity data, so faithfully collected since leaving the head of the Skelton Glacier, might well hold a clue. Pouring over the values of gravitational acceleration that had been taken every 5 km revealed, to their pleasure and amazement, that the gravity and seismic data were in agreement. Both sets of data were reflecting the same anomalies. And the chaotic ice surface appeared to confirm both. The gravity anomaly at this station, which is now known as the Wilkes Land Anomaly, was scores of times greater than the regional values elsewhere on the continent (Appendix B). Discoveries were now

---

[1]Brothers Wilbur and Orville Wright in 1903.

Figure 8.1. Arnie and Al, working on the pit wall.

Figure 8.2. Lou, taking a sun shot.

accumulating, consequences of persistence, time, and distance. The VLT team was again proving its worth, however trying the journey had been.

After supper, Tommy, Al, Frans, Jack, and Bill remained in Mess Cat talking over the usual traverse matters, and enjoying the camaraderie. Arnie and Lou did not join in, going instead to Detector, where they busied themselves writing up their work. Lou was very conscientious about his navigating, a huge responsibility (Fig. 8.2). Frans and Jack decided to share their discoveries about the anomaly with Tommy, Al, and Bill. Once they heard the full description, including the scientific significance of these observations, they too were elated. Questions and answers abounded until 2215, when they all hit the sack. At 2300, the temperature had warmed to −22 °C (−7.6 °F) with a gentle 1 knot (1.15 mph) wind.

On Sunday, December 20, Jack and Frans were busy making seismic shots with Nitramon explosives. Removing the ice cores with care, to preserve their use for glaciological and isotopic analyses, they delivered them to Al, Arnie, and Claude (Fig. 8.3). Claude's isotope analyses and Al and Arnie's glaciological analyses would have implications for global climatic change. Data such as these would be significant in later discoveries by Jack and Al relating to European historic and cartographic records that ultimately led to a revision of the date of discovery of Antarctica by some three centuries (Appendix C).[2] The VLT team was now in the region where Sir Douglas Mawson's Australasian Antarctic Expedition of 1911–1912 endured its trials, where Lieutenant Belgrave Ninnis and Xavier Mertz of Mawson's Far Eastern party lost their lives, and where the expedition discovered and mapped the Mertz and Ninnis Glaciers. Their contributions would be the basis for work years later by Jack, Al, and Frans regarding the origin and collapse of the Mertz and Ninnis Glacier Tongues on the coast of the Southern Ocean. The VLT team's discoveries continued to mount, some made years after these predecessors', and after the end of the traverse.

Arnie and Al continued digging their pit, finishing at 1330. After lunch, Detector departed, followed later by Seismo and Mess Cat. By the end of the day, the VLT team had made nine miles, stopping for the day at 1810. During the evening radio schedule, it was learned that a P2V had been tasked to make the airdrop. Tomorrow or the next day the traverse would reach B-61, Apex Depot, VLT Station 531. That evening at supper the team listened again to *Family Corner* from New Zealand, enjoying some contact with the outside world.

On Monday, December 21, everyone was up at 0730, in anticipation of reaching Apex Depot. It was a clear and sunny day with a wind of 10 knots (12 mph) and a temperature of −26 °C (−14.8 °F). By afternoon the wind had increased to 15 knots (17 mph). The past few days Frans had been riding on Seismo's sled or lying on a mattress on top of Seismo, sunning himself. Tommy had been riding on Mess Cat's sled. Both Tommy and

Frans sometimes walked along beside the sled for exercise, while Bill rode the banana sled behind Mess Cat. They all tended, in the polar sun, to fall asleep.

Very near completing the first leg, the longest leg of the Victoria Land Traverse, the team was in high spirits. B-61, Apex Depot, was less than thirty miles away. Whether the traverse would be able to travel beyond that station or not, it would at least be possible to join the scientific data to those of the French ALT. The VLT got under way after breakfast and made 15 miles by ~1430. Spotting a line of trail flags, the team had found the second fuel airdrop cache. Not unlike the first, this airdrop would prove to be 16 km from its reported location. Again the team was fortunate, far more fortunate than Captain Robert Falcon Scott and his team, who fell short a few brief miles from their next cache—and therefore perished in March 1912.

Following the trail flags to the fuel cache, the VLT team found sixty-four drums of fuel on sixteen pallets, 3,200 gallons total. The traverse would be able to continue, but the SnoCats and

Figure 8.3. Jack, with ice cores from drilling seismic shot holes. These ice cores were analyzed by Al, Arnie, and Claude for glaciological and isotope studies.

sleds would have heavier loads to tow. There was renewed concern about equipment failures. The added weight would stress the vehicles and sleds substantially. The fuel drums and pallets would be extracted from the snow the next day, and loaded onto sleds. The Rolligon, however, was refueled partly until 2230. The team then relaxed in Mess Cat, each member hydrating himself with water and, after some brief conversation, most headed exhausted for their sleeping bags. A short time later, Frans and Jack retired, too.

The next morning, Tuesday, December 22, the wind was 20–23 knots (23–26 mph), but by afternoon it would decrease to 10 knots (12 mph). The weather was warm, –23 °C (–9.4 °F), with clouds in all directions. The team set to work quickly. The Rolligon was filled by 0900. It took 600 gallons. There were thirteen drums of fuel left from the last fuel cache, so the VLT appeared to have sufficient fuel for the rest of the traverse to make it to the end. The team breathed a sigh of relief, mindful however of the challenges ahead. As on the first leg of the journey, the sastrugi would be oriented perpendicular to the trail on the second leg. That meant more rough riding when the traverse headed east toward the Ross Sea and the Transantarctic Mountains. The question "Could the equipment handle it?" arose again. Frans recognized that they might never reach the Tucker Glacier. Al and Arnie believed the sastrugi would damage the equipment so severely that the team would not reach the glacier. Thus far the VLT had traveled 1,560 km (975 miles). Al suggested that the team strive to travel 1,000 km (600 miles) more, and at least until January. Frans and Jack agreed, urging farther, if possible.

Detector left at 0900, this time for Apex Depot, 10 km ahead, without its sled. Seismo turned and headed back one station to recalibrate the gravimeter. Mess Cat went on ahead at 0945 and, after three stations, stopped. Detector had turned around, because it had learned that Seismo had broken its left-front tie-rod end. The supply of tie-rod ends, pontoon bearings, and fifth wheels was now exhausted. Detector stayed at a station one stop away from Seismo and Mess Cat, so Al and Arnie missed dinner. After dinner, Mess Cat traveled ahead to join Detector. Tommy was driving, so Claude and Bill jumped into their sleeping bags. Seismo remained behind because Seismo and Detector had to read their altimeters at the same time each day in order to create a continuous altimetric record. On the radio schedule that night, NAF McMurdo advised that a P2V would take off at 0900 the next day, making an airdrop of spare parts, parts that were badly needed.

On December 23, there was a light wind and partly cloudy skies; the temperature was –28.5 °C (–19.3 °F). At breakfast Lou complained that he was going home no matter what. No one knew how he planned to accomplish this. Tommy said that if the P2V landed, he was getting on it. Arnie was unhappy with the breakfast: "Oats again!" Claude and Jack were the only ones not complaining. The real barometer of the team's attitude was that everyone laughed, knowing that the complaints were meant to blow off steam. By 1530, Frans was in radio contact with the P2V, #40436, which arrived at the team's location at 1630, dropping

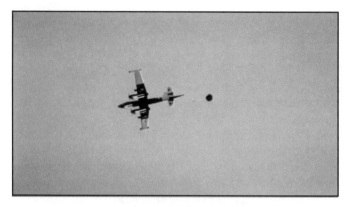

Figure 8.4. P2V, making its airdrops.

eight 'chutes of gear. The plane took 30–40 min to make the airdrop (Fig. 8.4). Their aim was good, most of the parachutes landing close to the camp. Arnie ran after the 'chutes as they reached the ground, retrieving and hustling back to camp with whatever he could carry. All of the team members pitched in, bringing the airdropped boxes and packages to the camp and quickly opening them (Fig. 8.5). Spare parts, food, and mail (Fig. 8.6) were the prized contents of the drop. As usual, everyone was excited, happy, and talking. Spirits soared.

Figure 8.5. Jack and Al, unpacking one of the airdropped boxes—this one the "goodie box," with mail and "refreshments."

Figure 8.6. Jack, sorting the mail and spare parts.

The P2V made a low pass over the SnoCats, tilting its wings in recognition, then flew south and east. The U.S. Navy's VX-6 Squadron was a God send. While the VLT team was prepared to do whatever it took to complete the journey, it had been impossible to carry sufficient fuel, spare parts, and provisions for a journey of the length proposed. Human endurance was adequate to the task, but not the vehicles. The VX-6 airdrops were essential. And while the crews and aircraft had thus far made their flights to the VLT without accident, it was not widely known that the squadron endured scores of accidents and loss of personnel in the years when we were there. They did their jobs well. The VLT team honored, respected, and relied upon these men, without whom the traverse would not have achieved Apex Depot. The length of the remaining leg of the journey was still in doubt, but the support of VX-6 Squadron was not.

The most sought-after item was mail. In addition, several bottles of spirits had been included in the drop. John Russell sent a bottle of Benedictine liqueur, while a Kiwi friend of the VLT team, Mary Pat Gamble, sent a bottle of scotch for Bill. Also included were fresh vegetables, coffee, rolls, tomatoes, and, of course, spare parts for the vehicles. Paperback books, cookies, magazines, and signs reading "Next Week We've Got to Get Organized" were also included. There was a Christmas card from Stephen "Denny" Den Hartog, who had been on the traverse from Little America the year before with Bert Crary and Bucky Wilson. For about an hour there was reading and silence, broken only by exclamations, chuckles, and the exchange of bits of information from the letters. At dinner it was agreed that this was the best airdrop ever. For dinner Bill served up scrambled eggs, bacon, and light drinks. Conscious of the season, Christmas carols were played on the tape recorder, and the group sang some of them. Christmas was clearly in the air. It snowed that afternoon and evening.

That evening, NAF McMurdo relayed to the VLT team a message from VX-6:

P2V on drop of December 23 flew track 067 degrees to 47 degrees from Hallet station to your (VLT) position. Recon of terrain en route. Pilots and navigator report zone of crevasses on their course between 141 and 142 degrees East at 71 degrees 40 minutes South. Consist of a series of numerous crevasses or rifts perpendicular across track and extending out of sight. Rifts described as one and three quarters to mile and one half wide. Rifts appeared to be one hundred to three hundred feet wide with sheer walls perhaps 30 to 40 feet high. Plane radar got good returns at 20 miles. Some crevasses to true north bridged, some not. Suggestion that attempt to bypass rifts be made to true south since you met nothing on your track to station B61. Mountainous area west of Hallet much more extensive than charted. First mountains you will come to lie between 161 and 162 degrees oriented north and south extending to horizons. Peaks estimated to 9,000 plus feet with heavy crevassing at bases. Beyond there to true east is area of thirty miles of crevasses before next mountains. Impenetrable mountainous area to coast. Plan recon of area prior your arrival, but suggest no vehicle penetration beyond first mountains. Russian traverse sighted heading to the Pole....

This news was unexpected! The traverse to our last airdropped fuel cache had seemed crevasse-free. The team had unknowingly "threaded the needle" on the way to Apex Depot (Fig. 8.7), again avoiding catastrophe. The chaotic ice terrain that Frans and Jack observed implied that strange things were going on beneath the ice. And their seismic and gravity data confirmed it. The presence of sizeable basins and troughs in the ice surface were related to the crevasse fields reported by the P2V. The areas with huge crevasses, some open and some with substantial snow bridges, seen immediately north and south of the VLT track, were areas that the team never could have crossed. Rapid and stressed movement in the continental ice sheet created the unusually large crevasses, the stress the result of the complex subglacial topography revealed by the seismic and gravity

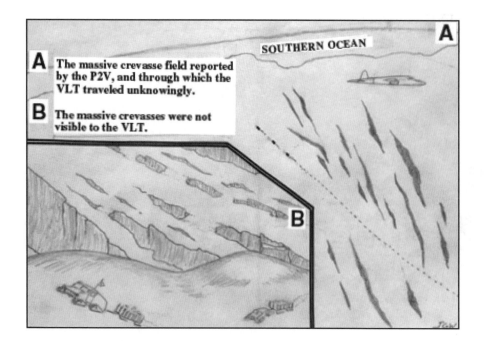

Figure 8.7. *Threading the needle*. The VLT team, unaware of the substantial crevasse fields both north and south of its trail, was unable to photograph the crevasses that were out of sight. **A** depicts the regional picture reported by the P2V, and the dotted line depicts the trail of the VLT team's traverse. **B** depicts a close-up view of the crevasses that were not visible from the SnoCats.

surveys. Jack and Frans believed that these features were likely accompanied by ice streams in the vicinity of the traverse, ice streams that with the complex subglacial topography accounted for the chaotic ice surface (Appendix D).

In spite of the risky conditions in the vicinity of the VLT, it was a fine day. Detector had found B-61 at 1430, 2.4 km (1.5 miles) east of the traverse course, the end point of the ALT of the year before that had begun 300 km north at Charcot. Finding the pole left by Claude's French traverse the year before (Fig. 8.8) was like finding a needle in a haystack! The success was due to outstanding navigating by Lou. The identifying pole was 3 m (9.8 ft.) tall, orange in color, and bearing a tattered tricolor French flag with a can attached to the pole. The can contained a note (Fig. 8.9) that Claude read and treasured.

On December 24, Christmas Eve day, there was a 10 knot (11 mph) wind and a temperature of −24 °C (−11.2 °F). In the morning, Arnie and Al dug 3 m (9.8 ft.) of their pit. Jack and Frans drilled a deep seismic shot hole, and laid out geophone cable for seismic recording. Work stopped for Christmas Eve dinner at 1700. Jack and Bill had prepared the dinner table with food from the airdrop, including cigars left by the evacuated Taylor (Fig. 8.10). Cocktail hour, two hours long, was highlighted by martinis, except for Frans and Lou, who preferred thawed-out beer.

The main course was thawed steak with side dishes of cheese and nuts. Al got slightly inebriated, so much so that he did not eat dinner and instead ventured outside for air. Trying to rejoin the group, Al mistook the rear doors of Mess Cat for the "main entrance," attempting unsuccessfully to enter. The

Figure 8.8. Claude and the pole at B-61 left by him and his French colleagues on the previous year's Adélie Land Traverse.

Figure 8.9. Jack, Al, Lou, and Claude at the French station, B-61, VLT Station 531, Apex Depot.

tool box and Claude's bunk lay across the opening. Al attacked the tools and the bunk, strewing tools on the snow. Clearly in a festive mood, the team took Al's performance gracefully and sympathetically. Al, seeming nonetheless to be in the Christmas spirit, headed for Detector, and went to bed. Dinner was followed by music and light conversation. Bill suggested that they have a party in Christchurch, New Zealand, when the traverse was over. Jack suggested that the group wear their parkas, and have the party on the banks of the lovely River Avon in Christchurch—in the park. The group enthusiastically nodded their approval. Lou announced that he had decided that he would spend a couple

of weeks in Tahiti on the way home. Jack planned on driving from the West Coast to Wisconsin, and Tommy, Claude, and Bill decided to join him. The group then lapsed into song until they went to bed at midnight.

On Friday, December 25, Christmas Day, there was a 15 knot (17 mph) wind, a temperature of −24 °C (−11.2 °F), and it was cloudy. Frans was up first at 0800. The rest slept until 0900. Al was a bit worse for wear from the previous night's party. It was decided nonetheless that because it was the holiday season, and because the VLT had achieved Apex Depot, the team deserved song and celebration. Jack and Al prepared martinis, and the

Figure 8.10. The VLT team's Christmas Eve dinner table included (from the back) bread, libations, apples, nuts, cheese, cigars, and "cookie remnants." Because no martini glasses were available, tripe was discarded from small jars; then the jars (at right) were washed with snow and used for the "Yuletide" cocktails.

Figure 8.11. At B-61, Station 531, Apex Depot. Photo taken after "singing in the snow." Note the smiles. Front row: Al, Lou, Jack, and Tommy. Back row: Frans, Claude, Arnie, and Bill.

team retired to the soft snow outside, sitting in a circle. They drank and toasted one another. Still in the holiday spirit, Tommy started singing. Al, slightly disapproving of Tommy's choices, reminded all that this was Christmas, and suggested religious songs. Jack suggested "Jesus Loves Me" ("this I know, 'cause the Bible tells me so"). The singing continued until the second glass was dry. Now in pretty good spirits, it was next agreed, because the team members were deserving and such impressive adventurers, that they should celebrate further by taking a family picture. The team, assembled around the ALT French flag pole, straightened their attire, and smiled for posterity (Fig. 8.11). All

were quite certain we'd be pleased with the outcome, once we'd seen the photo.

Christmas though it was, Frans and Lou took off in Detector at 1100 to go back 12 miles on the trail to prepare to make a refraction detonation the next day. Jack in the meantime prepared to record the seismic shot in Seismo. Jack, Al, and Arnie slept in Seismo, while Bill, Claude, and Tommy drove back in Mess Cat to join Frans and Lou in Detector, until the next day.

On Saturday, December 26, Frans radioed from Detector that they were unable to start their engines. So Jack drove back in Seismo, joining Detector and Mess Cat at B-61. Al, Arnie, and

Figure 8.12. The pole at B-61 as the VLT team left it, surrounded by empty fuel drums covered with parachutes. The site, though looking forlorn, was decorated—the pole wrapped in Christmas tinsel—and intended as a cheerful welcome to later explorers who might follow. Now, however, a half century later, Apex Depot resides well beneath the snow, in the East Antarctic continental ice sheet.

Claude went back with Jack, and then transferred to Mess Cat. Seismo would serve as a radio relay to Mess Cat, and Jack would fire the seismic refraction shot. However, it turned out that Frans had fired the shot the previous day without radio contact, so no data were recorded in Seismo, and the effort was wasted. Jack was not pleased. Seismo left ~1100 with Claude, Arnie, and Al. As a safety measure, they were to call Mess Cat every 15 min. Tommy, Jack, and Bill now stayed with Mess Cat; at 1700, Jack made radio contact with Frans, and then detonated the seismic shot. The refraction shot this time was successful, and the day of musical SnoCats came to an end! Mess Cat then drove back to join Seismo and Detector. There was therefore, on occasion, some inefficiency born of fatigue and miscommunication.

Though it had been a pleasant change of pace at Apex Depot, with the airdrop, Christmas holiday, libations, good food and song, albeit laced with some confusion, the time had come to resume the traverse. With Detector in the lead, the traverse team now headed east. Seismo and Mess Cat labored under the weight of the new fuel drums on their sleds, and the reloaded Rolligon. Apex Depot retained the orange French pole and tattered flag, surrounded by empty fuel drums (Fig. 8.12), remaining a potentially useful point for later scientific exploration.

Chapter 9

Into SnoCat no-man's land

While the holiday change of pace had been mood elevating for the entire VLT team, it was apparent to everyone that even greater challenges remained, if the traverse was to be completed successfully. Frans expressed doubt that the traverse would go the full distance to the Tucker Glacier. The condition of the vehicles and sleds and the probability of more devastating sastrugi were of great concern. No one, especially the planners, had anticipated the challenges the group would face. Some wondered if it was an impossible journey! There was still, however, considerable resolve among most members of the team. Experience with equipment failures on the first half of the journey suggested that the vehicles and sleds were very near the end of their usefulness. The traverse team had escaped having to abandon either SnoCats or sleds because of Tommy's skill and the team's determination. But the condition of the equipment now made the outcome doubtful. Beyond that, the December 23 message from the VX-6 P2V was unexpected. The team thought it had crossed comparatively safe terrain, apart from the damaging sastrugi. It now appeared that it might face threatening crevasse country more severe than anything encountered previously. Crevasses and crevasse fields of the magnitude where the VLT "threaded the needle" lay directly to the east, along the traverse's planned route of travel (Appendix D). It was something of a miracle that the inbound route taken to Apex Depot passed through the massive crevasse field without knowledge or incident.

The question now was whether to attempt to negotiate the crevasse fields in the traverse's path, or to somehow circumvent them. Frans led the discussion. It was his opinion that the traverse should proceed directly at the crevasse field to the north of its previous track, and Jack agreed. This plan would offer several advantages: (1) it was the shorter of any alternate routes; (2) it would provide an opportunity to observe perhaps the largest crevasses on the planet and to determine their exact sizes and configurations; and (3) it would provide the opportunity to experience yet one more adventure. They were alone. None of the other members of the team was prepared to risk the remainder of the journey on such a plan. The matter was discussed at great length and for some time. It was eventually agreed to take the advice of the P2V crew and avoid the crevasse fields to the north

and south. This meant retracing the VLT track into Apex Depot (Fig. 9.1). It meant driving back to the southeast, over the trail that had encountered no crevasses, to a point at which the traverse could avoid the crevasse fields to the north and south. And then head due east. Al ventured, "No more sleeping at the wheel!"

After departing Station B-61, Mess Cat broke the pin off the right end of the front spreader bar on its sled. Tommy was unable to fit the new one. So instead, as previously done on Detector's sled, Tommy put two bolts through the tow bar and runners, hoping this would do the trick. On Sunday, December 27, the

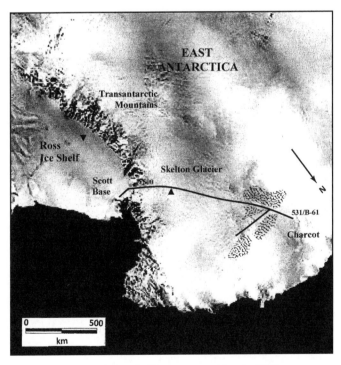

Figure 9.1. The track into B-61 was retraced by the VLT team, eastward from Station B-61. Backtracking 64 km (40 miles) would enable the traverse to avoid the crevassing to the north and south reported by the Navy P2V. The ▼ symbol marks the location of the Kiwis' crevasse accident. The ▲ symbol identifies the location of the VLT team when the Kiwis' radio call for help was intercepted.

Figure 9.2. Sastrugi, east of Apex Depot, after the VLT team cleared the region of chaotic ice.

morning was warm, with a temperature of −27 °C (−16.6 °F). With a 10 knot (11.5 mph) wind, at 0915 Detector returned to the stop 1.2 km (0.75 miles) away where it had left its sled. As it did so, the front tie-rod end broke. Mess Cat joined Detector when Tommy discovered Mess Cat's sled had broken, the bed having pulled off the rear runners. It took from 0950 to 1415 to repair the sled, and Seismo delivered a spare tie-rod end to Detector. The sastrugi had not improved. Bill bet Claude a beer that the traverse would not make it much farther, and that the VLT team would need to be airlifted within four weeks. Everyone became quiet, wondering again if it was an impossible journey. During dinner the group listened to the New Zealand radio broadcast *Family Corner* on frequency 11780. Frans and Lou discussed where it would be necessary to turn east off our trail to avoid crevasses. They agreed that it would be wise to backtrack at least forty miles before turning east, just before reaching the bowl-shaped depression we'd passed on the way in to B-61.

Frans and Jack continued to puzzle over several anomalies that had been discovered, and again came to the conclusion that the chaotic ice surface, which now included also the fields of anomalously large crevasses and snow bridges in the vicinity of the basins, troughs, and huge rollers, were caused by unusual subglacial topography. Jack was concerned that the altimetry data be preserved and sent to the University of Wisconsin, where he would tie it to the seismic and gravity data. The data would be needed in order to accurately profile not only the continental ice sheet surface, but the subglacial topography as well. The interpretation of the discoveries he and Frans were making would depend on this information as well as on the seismic and gravity data. Because ice, like all deformable materials, normally seeks its own level, the presence of basins and troughs in the ice surface suggested that they resulted from relatively recent glaciological activity. In the evening, Tommy and Claude took sponge baths because both believed the traverse was nearly over. Claude was

also apprehensive because upon his return to France, he would be required to go back into the army for fifteen months.

The next morning was Monday, December 28. The temperature had remained fairly constant the past few days. After breakfast, material on Mess Cat's sled was repacked, and food thought to be in excess of what would be needed was offloaded and placed in a cache. Chocolate bars, one case of coffee, two cases of Pream (a nondairy creamer), graham crackers, mozzarella cheese, one box of fruit cake, nuts, and cheese would be left behind. After dinner, Frans, Tommy, and Arnie tried welding a crack in Detector's frame. The sleds too continued to show serious signs of wear.

On December 29, the temperature was −25 °C (−13 °F), clear, sunny, and with a 10 knot (11.5 mph) wind. At 1530, Seismo broke the rear spreader bar on its sled. Mess Cat broke its right-rear pontoon bearing, and a short time later the left-rear spring on Mess Cat broke completely in half. The SnoCats and sleds continued to succumb to the chaotic sastrugi surface. Clouds began moving in around 1800, and by 2345, the sky was overcast.

On December 30, everyone was up by 0800. The sky was clear and sunny, and there was an 8 knot (6.9 mph) wind and a temperature of −24 °C (−11.2 °F). After Detector's departure, Seismo and Mess Cat had just started out when Detector radioed the news that it had broken the rear spreader bar on its sled. The sastrugi remained unrelenting (Fig. 9.2). Al remarked, "When we get back and talk about this over a martini, it will seem funny." Jack said, "It seems funny now." Al replied, "I know, something like a Mack Sennett comedy and that's what's frightening."[1] Tommy, Jack, and

---

[1]Mack Sennett (January 17, 1880–November 5, 1960) is "widely regarded as the father of slapstick for his pioneering silent film work as an actor, director and producer during cinema's earliest days" (Mack Sennett—The Father of Slapstick Cinema, http://www.legacy.com/ns/news-story.aspx?t=mack-sennett--the-father-of-slapstick-cinema&id=152, accessed March 6, 2012).

Figure 9.3. Seismo and Mess Cat proceed through falling snow.

Al rigged a spreader bar made of a wooden beam from the crevasse detector, since there were no more spares. Frans and Claude went back 3.2 km (2 miles) to recalibrate the gravimeter.

The traverse passed through a large trough that day, descending 43 m (141 ft.), reminiscent of the region of chaotic ice terrain and the basins and troughs seen in the west. Despite the deteriorating condition of the vehicles and sleds, the team remained resolved. A few days earlier, Claude had said that he was sad that the traverse was almost at an end. Then he received a telegram on the evening radio schedule from his girlfriend back in France. Suddenly, he had an epiphany, advising the group he was now "ready to go home!"

Thursday, December 31, was New Year's Eve and was certain to include a celebration. We made 19 km (12 miles) that day in 10 h. It snowed all day in a whiteout (Fig. 9.3). We stopped at 1800 because of poor visibility. At one of the stations during a pause in our progress, Claude, Jack, Tommy, and Bill reflected on the meals, the food, and other rations that had been provided. All agreed that improvements were needed. The sameness, perhaps unavoidable, was a problem. There was more chocolate than needed. During the entire traverse the team had not gone through one case of chocolate. But, in defense of the planners, the team had made few suggestions. Jack felt that dense heavy foods were most often preferred—beans, Beefaroni, canned meat, and pemmican (a high-calorie paste of dried and pounded meat mixed with other ingredients including melted fat).

Frans, listening, agreed. But, he'd been thinking about the trail ahead. Frans believed 320 km (200 miles) could be the maximum the traverse would get out of the equipment. It could be necessary to construct an airstrip and call for evacuation. Because of the sastrugi, an airstrip would likely be impossible.

The traverse stopped for the day at 1800. At the previous stop, Tommy had suggested to Frans that the next day should be a holiday—New Year's Day. Frans, upon reflection, noted that on Christmas Day at Station B-61 the team took no holiday, but went about its work as usual. Frans continued, "Well, we've been traveling much too slowly, and we still have far to go. I'd be inclined to say no." As soon as we stopped for the day, Tommy asked the rest of the team if they thought New Year's Day should be a holiday. Most agreed, except for Jack and Al, who felt that, if it was good weather, we should travel. At dinner, after some discussion and while Frans was on the radio, a vote was taken. After listening to the arguments, everyone was in favor of continuing the traverse except for Lou. After dinner, Frans, Arnie, and Al left Mess Cat, while Jack, Claude, Bill, Tommy, and Lou (who was doing dishes) stayed and listened to music. It became a consolation party, a small New Year's Eve celebration before we hit the trail the next day. We tried, unsuccessfully, to sing "Auld Lang Syne."

The next morning, the temperature was −25 °C (−13 °F), with a 25–30 knot (29–35 mph) wind. The sleds were drifted over (Fig. 9.4), and the traverse began a little late. Those in Detector

Figure 9.4. Drifting snow from a blizzard covers Mess Cat's sled.

cleaned out the vehicle. Bill dried out his mukluks in front of Mess Cat's heater. Jack took a sponge bath and washed his hair.

Dinner that evening was at 2030. During dinner, Claude presented each of us with a French medal, a lapel pin awarded to those who have ventured to one of the poles, and who have made significant contributions to polar exploration and research (Fig. 9.5). Each of us was now an honorary member of *Expedition Polaire Française.* (Claude had received permission from Paul-Émile Victor, head of the French polar program, to award the pin to members of the Victoria Land Traverse.) It was a kind and much appreciated gesture. A year later, the United States issued its Antarctic Service Medal.

That evening the talk turned inevitably to equipment breakdown, sastrugi, and the probability or not of completing the traverse. It was Frans' judgment that one hundred to two hundred miles was the maximum the VLT could make. His opinion would be justified by the events that lay ahead, although the result was still uncertain. Lou believed fifty miles was the most that we could make. Though it would be crowded, the traverse could continue with two SnoCats and one sled, if the other equipment should fail. An advantage, Jack pointed out, was that abandoned equipment could be cannibalized, and the parts used to bolster the remaining SnoCats and sleds.

The previous day, the SnoCats and sleds descended 59 m (193 ft.) into another ice surface basin, a repeat of our experience of a few days ago, confirmation of the anomalous condition of the continental ice sheet in the vicinity. Jack and Frans again examined their notes from the day before and the seismic and gravity data. The subglacial topography was the fundamental part of the puzzle[2] (Appendix E). By 2420, the temperature reached −22.5 °C (−8.5 °F), but in a blizzard. The wind had increased to 30 knots (34 mph) with gusts to 40 knots (46 mph). Visibility was restricted, and the 'Cats and sleds were under heavy drifting.

January 2 was a day of lying in. There was little choice. The wind was blowing at 30–35 knots (34–40 mph), and it was snowing. The temperature was −22 °C (−7.6 °F). The sun was not visible; so it was not possible to navigate. At 2230, the temperature warmed to −17 °C (+1.4 °F). Frans, understandably uncertain, was faced with the dilemma that we might be able to see the sun but not the surface due to blowing snow. Should we resume travel or not if we faced those conditions the next day? Our progress

had been slow; we had many miles yet to travel. Jack favored travel, as did Frans and a majority of the team.

January 3 would be a travel day. The temperature was warm, with a 5 knot (6 mph) wind, although the sky was still heavily overcast, and the sun barely visible, but still in whiteout. The traverse team drove all day, slowed constantly by rough sastrugi. At 1745, Seismo broke its front universal joint. It was repaired in 45 minutes. Then the spreader bar on the rear of Detector's sled, the jury-rigged wood beam, also broke. At dinner, Lou and Frans had a brief altercation, at Lou's instigation. Sitting and sulking, not saying a word, he unexpectedly erupted. "How about parking the SnoCat next time so I don't have to move my tripod? This makes the third time that's happened. You talk about cooperation, but you don't cooperate." Frans responded, "Okay, next time you guide me while I'm parking." Lou was not quite satisfied with this response and kept on. Frans responded well, and Lou went back to sulking. At 2130, the wind was blowing ~15 knots (17 mph) with gusts to 20 knots (23 mph). Visibility improved only slightly. It was still a whiteout. The temperature was −18 °C (−0.4 °F). If we were able to make 24 km (15 miles) the next day as we had done on this day, then Tuesday, January 5, would be a station day.

The next day was January 4 and Tommy's twenty-third birthday. Detector got under way at 0900. At 1030, Seismo broke its right-rear spring. The sun was shining weakly through the overcast. The wind decreased to 15 knots (17 mph). At 1815, our last

Figure 9.5. The silver medal Claude gave to each of the VLT team, a tribute from *Expédition Polaire Française.* The VLT team were now members of *Expédition Polaire Française.*

<hr>

[2]Upon return to the Geophysical and Polar Research Center at the University of Wisconsin, Jack would examine in much greater detail the significance of the chaotic ice, the subglacial topography, and the seismic and gravity evidence. He concluded that the subglacial structure resembled craterform topography, and published his hypothesis in 1976. His later work (Appendix E) resulted in the structure being classified on the Impact Database as a "possible" impact crater. In 2010, after considerably more research and the availability of new radiosound and satellite remote sensing data, Jack and Frans published an updated glaciological, subglacial, and geophysical analysis, concluding that the structure was indeed both craterform and larger than originally postulated (Weihaupt and Van der Hoeven, 2004a, 2004b, 2006; Weihaupt et al., 2010). The Impact Database reclassified the structure on the basis of this paper as a "probable" impact structure. The anomalies they had discovered were finally making sense.

Figure 9.6. Seismo's broken trailer hitch.

station for the day, Seismo broke its trailer hitch (Fig. 9.6). After the jury-rig repair, the traverse drove in whiteout all day, with a wall of clouds 30–61 m (100–200 ft.) around us in all directions. We made 22 km (14 miles) that day.

At dinner, the discussion turned again to the driving conditions and equipment failures. We had been averaging only 16–24 km (10–15 miles) a day since we'd left Apex Depot on December 26. Running perpendicular to the sastrugi, the vehicles and sleds were suffering all the more. At this rate of travel, the VLT team might not reach the mountains, much less the Ross Sea Coast. The sun continued to descend lower to the horizon. That left two alternatives. First, do twelve more major stations and run the risk of not reaching the mountains or, second, do six more major stations driving 3–4 days between major stations and reaching the mountains, if possible. Jack, Frans, and Bill favored the first alternative—Continue as we're doing, determined we'll make it anyway. Al and Claude favored the second approach. Arnie and Lou had left Mess Cat when the discussion started and did not participate. Jack nevertheless reemphasized the importance of reaching the mountains. They had never been seen from the ground, nor plotted. It would be a major contribution to the scientific world. Not only that—reaching them might provide an opportunity to climb a mountain and make some geological observations. Al and Claude believed that it was important to get as many glaciological pits dug as possible for continuity, although Claude noted that his work did not require so many stations. Jack said he felt obliged to make as many seismic stations and gravity observations as possible, but he felt they'd be justified in reducing the number, if it meant reaching the mountains. He believed that the mere rough mapping and plotting of a new mountain range was most important. Al then agreed. Tommy understandably felt that driving straight for the mountains would be too hard on the equipment and cause more

breakdowns, but Jack and Al pointed out that breakdowns would occur regardless of which alternative was selected. Another factor to consider was that "management" might decide that the VLT team could not proceed, and that we should be evacuated before we had a chance to reach the mountains. Al observed that if we were to do only six stations and then find we needed to wait two weeks for evacuation, we would have lost the valuable opportunity to carry out the scientific observations from here to the mountains. Jack pointed out that there was a great deal of work that could yet be done from that point to the mountains, and again once in the mountains. Not only that, the team might consider man-hauling the banana sled and equipment to explore further, once within the mountains.

The question then arose regarding Seismo's broken trailer hitch, and the fact that it would be unlikely that Seismo could continue much farther under its great load. And Detector's main frame had broken! It was decided that the Rolligon would be towed by Mess Cat, and that Seismo's sled must be lightened. The material removed would be distributed to Mess Cat insofar as possible, and the remainder left on the trail as a cache for any future travelers. It was determined further, to the consternation of all, that Detector and its sled would need to be abandoned. With its broken mainframe, it could not continue; but would be cannibalized for spare parts for the remaining two SnoCats. At 2345, the temperature was −19 °C (−2.2 °F) with a 5–10 knot (6–12 mph) wind. The sky had cleared directly overhead, although around us the wall of clouds prevailed, extending to the surface. The mood was serious, with thoughts of potentially abandoning Detector, which had become part of the "family."

On Tuesday, January 5, the sky was overcast, but it was now possible to see the horizon. The wind was 5 knots (6 mph), and the temperature −16 °C (+3.2 °F). The team slept until 0900. Al and Arnie got to work on the pit and dug 1 m (3.3 ft.) by breakfast time. The pit was finished by 1620, and the core provided by Frans and Jack was analyzed by 1730. Frans and Jack drilled holes for seismic shots, spread the heavy cable of the geophones, and made the detonations and recordings. The seismic reflections were the best they had gotten to date, so they were both elated. Claude managed to collect selected samples from the drill cores for his isotopic analyses. After breakfast, the sled loads were rearranged. The overcast cleared by 1330, and the temperature warmed to −10 °C (+14 °F), with a one knot wind. A beautiful day, it was a very pleasant interlude, and both Claude and Bill shaved. Dinner was early, at 1730; then the team repacked the sleds and moved the Rolligon to Mess Cat. Seismo would pull only its lightened sled. The team then milled about on this "warm," pleasant evening.

The VLT team arose at 0800 the next morning. The conversation revolved around, strangely, bees, snakes, and spiders. The discussion was not very scientific or polar, and the traverse set off soon thereafter. At 1200, Seismo broke the rear spreader bar on its sled. At 1530, the bottom rail on the right-rear pontoon of Detector tore off, and the track began running under rather than over the rail (Fig. 9.7). The traverse stopped for repairs. While repairs were being made, Al and Arnie worked on their pit data from Station 536. The average accumulation there was found to be higher than usual, 21+ cm of water equivalent.

Our position was 143°54′E, 72°06′S. The surface continued to be extremely rough, the sastrugi still perpendicular to our travel. Mess Cat, now pulling the Rolligon and its heavier sled, drove full throttle and in second gear. The banging and careening continued to be devastating to what was left of the vehicles and sleds. Three more points were found on the lower rails of Detector's pontoons where the rails were being worn away. That day the traverse made 19 km (12 miles). There was at that point some doubt we would make more than 24 km

(15 miles) per day. At that rate, it would take twenty days to reach the mountains, 480 km (300 miles) to the east. If we made it to the mountains, it was unlikely to happen until the end of January. It was also a race against time as the sun was setting lower in the sky. Winter was not far off. At 2215, the temperature was −22 °C (−7.6 °F) with a 2–4 knot (2.3–5 mph) wind; the sky was clear and sunny.

On Thursday, January 7, Claude and Jack returned to Mess Cat after breakfast to read their notes and write before hitting the trail. At the first station, the front spreader bar on Seismo's sled broke. At 1430, Detector lost its right-rear sled runner. It was 1730 before repairs were made; so the traverse stopped for the evening. With the breakdowns, the traverse made 16 km (10 miles) that day.

On Friday, January 8, by noon, the wind had risen to 20 knots (23 mph), the temperature was −29.5° (−21.1 °F). Soon on the trail, the rear spreader bar on Mess Cat's sled broke. Later the rear runners pulled out from under the sled. The VLT team was 141 km (88 miles) east of the turnoff point from our incoming track to Apex Depot. We were clear, we estimated, of the crevasse fields to north and south. Seismo and Mess Cat started at 1015 and went 6 m (20 ft.) before Mess Cat broke a front tie-rod end. Repairs were completed, and Seismo and Mess Cat got back on the trail at 1130. At 1415, Seismo broke its left-rear spring. The spring was replaced, and Seismo continued on at 1515, stopping for the day at 1700. Al and Arnie finished digging 2 m (6.6 ft.) in the pit and took photos of the stratigraphy by 1900. It was warm enough that they took off their parkas and sweaters and rolled up their sleeves. Unusual for Claude, he had not been in good spirits the past two days and was rather quiet. Arnie had taken note, mentioning that Claude was tired. So were we all. Frans had been riding on Seismo's sled while Jack drove. Frans said he did this to get a tan and for "other reasons," which were, Bill thought, related

Figure 9.7. Detector's track derailed.

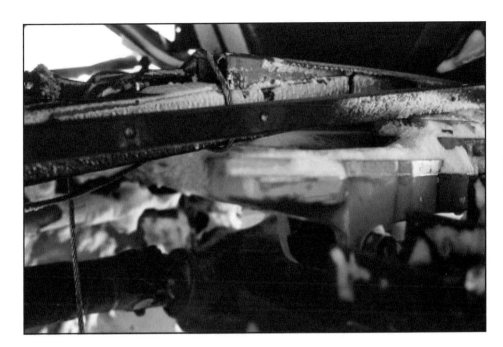

Figure 9.8. Broken frame on Detector. Tommy attempted to hold it with a wire wrap, but that failed.

to group dynamics. In the evening the team sat for a while after dinner, relaxing, talking, and having a beer, the last left in our inventory.

On Sunday, January 10, Bill was slow in getting up; so Al, Arnie, and Lou made their own breakfast. It was clear and sunny with a 15–17 mph wind and a temperature of –21 °C (–5.8 °F). Al and Arnie were in the pit by 1000 and finished it by 1430. Frans and Jack drilled holes for seismic shots, laid out the geophone lines, and detonated and recorded the seismic shots favoring anomalous gravity (Appendices F and G). Work at this major station was finished by 1600, so Detector left. Mess Cat and Seismo got under way at 1700. Al then changed his clothes, discarding a Norwegian wool sweater, wool shirt, red sweater, fish-net shirt, Byrd cloth windproofs, cotton shells, long johns, two pairs of socks, and bunny boots. He exchanged the boots for mukluks with two insoles inside each one.

Monday, January 11, was clear and sunny, with a 20 knot (23 mph) wind and a temperature of –28 °C (–18.4 °F). The chassis behind Detector's steering jack broke completely, twisting the rear portion of the chassis. This was accompanied by numerous cracks elsewhere near the chassis. Tommy used his "come along" (cable-jack) on the chassis. That didn't work. He then tried welding on the other side. That too failed. We had no way to make the repair. Sadly, Detector would likely need to be abandoned. At 2130, the temperature was –21 °C (–5.8 °F).

On Tuesday, January 12, there was not much conversation at breakfast, though there were scattered remarks about the likelihood that we would need to abandon Detector. The banana sled was disconnected from Detector and attached to Seismo. There was a 13 knot (15 mph) wind, and the temperature was –29 °C (–20.2 °F), with clear and sunny skies. Detector broke a front

tie-rod end, which required two hours to fix. Again it had a left-hand thread. In the spare parts box, we found only tie-rod ends with right-hand threads. Tommy split the end of the tie rod and attached it as best he could—his fingers cold and crossed. Bill fell ill at supper, caused, he thought, by constant jostling while traveling over sastrugi. The surface was now unusually rough and punishing, some of the sastrugi four feet high and hard as rock. Detector made it through the day with only a broken tie-rod end. Tommy, who had thought the 'Cat would break down completely, lost a beer bet to Claude (though all the beer was gone), who thought it would last until the next day.

On Wednesday, January 13, the traverse stopped for the day at 1600 after 18 km (11 miles) when Detector radioed saying they had another breakdown. Two of the SnoCat's tracks had unraveled from two pontoons. Even worse, the rear end of the 'Cat was badly sagging, tilted at an angle, and barely hanging on (Fig. 9.8). The pontoons too were out of line. Then the fifth wheel, we found, was tilted at an angle, with only one bracket holding, and it too was cracked (Fig. 9.9). The other brackets had already broken. Ironically, not much later, Seismo broke two track links. Al suggested that this stop be made a major station while repairs were being made, enabling him and Arnie to start another pit. Frans agreed, and team members set about their tasks, Jack and Frans preparing to make more reflection shots. There was a 15–25 knot (17–29 mph) wind, and the temperature was –25 °C (–13 °F). Claude paid Jack a nice compliment, exclaiming, "You are zee best driller I ever know!" Jack thanked Claude, and remembers Claude's compliment still.

Detector could go no farther. Some discussed the possibility of evacuation. Jack was not in favor of abandoning the traverse, of leaving all the 'Cats there together. Frans and Al

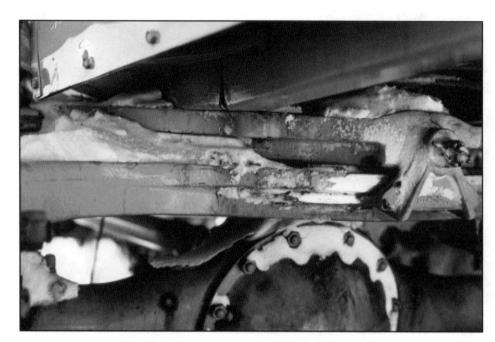

Figure 9.9. Broken chassis and fifth wheel on Detector.

Figure 9.10. Al was unhappy about abandoning "his" Detector.

Figure 9.11. Jack, offloading gear from Detector's sled, and reflecting on the status of the traverse and the team.

agreed. There was considerable sentiment for querying NAF McMurdo to get their opinions and instructions. The entire team, while remaining determined, was unsure of the rest of the equipment. With the sun beginning its descent and time growing short, our chances for achieving our final goal were looking questionable. A good deal of quiet contemplation was apparent. Al (Fig. 9.10), along with the rest of the team, suggested these were decisions that should not be made by us. NAF McMurdo should be made aware of the reality of our situation, and what was now an "improbable" journey. Jack (Fig. 9.11), while still reluctant to abandon the traverse, agreed that NAF McMurdo should be apprised of the situation and the lateness of the season. While Frans, Jack, Al, Arnie, and Claude were anxious to complete their scientific observations and extend them into the mountains, the challenges multiplied. As time and alternatives were dwindling, Arnie (Fig. 9.12) contemplated the chances of the traverse's—and our—survival, while Frans puzzled over the dwindling alternatives (Fig. 9.13).

Figure 9.12. Arnie, contemplating all the breakdowns and the fate of the VLT.

Figure 9.13. Frans, reflecting on the dire straits in which the Victoria Land Traverse now found itself. Al, background, is monitoring NAF radio frequency. The future looked bleak.

Chapter 10

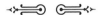

Abandonment — And discovery

At the evening radio schedule with NAF McMurdo, Frans, after describing the conditions of the vehicles and the terrain, returned to advise the team that Detector would go no farther. Detector would be cannibalized for its parts, and the Victoria Land Traverse would continue in two SnoCats, two sleds, and the Rolligon toward the mountains. A radio schedule was set for the following day at noon when the team would learn if NAF McMurdo had any further instructions or advice. Al and Arnie proceeded to dig a pit at 1530 and got 2 m (6.6 ft.) done before dinner. After dinner, Jack, Frans, and Claude drilled holes for seismic shots until all three were exhausted. The wind had blown hard all day, and by 2045, the temperature was −24 °C (−11.2 °F). In spite of the plight of the traverse, Jack and Frans' geophysical work was going well, as was Claude's isotopic research (Fig. 10.1).

On Thursday, January 14, it was clear and sunny. The wind was brisk at 12–18 knots (14–20 mph), and the temperature was −25 °C (−13 °F). The team arose at 1000, and attempted to contact NAF McMurdo at 1200, but couldn't raise them. We would try again that evening. None of the SnoCats would start that morning. Tommy put the Herman-Nelson heater on Seismo, got it started, then tried to start Mess Cat. No luck—so he then tried Detector. No luck. Tommy changed the points and coil in

Mess Cat, and still Mess Cat wouldn't start. He then changed the starter, put heated oil into the engine, and installed new spark plugs. Tommy didn't succeed in getting Mess Cat started until 2100, when Seismo arrived. Later Mess Cat's engine died, because its battery was dead. Seismo towed Mess Cat until, finally, its engine started.

Al and Arnie finished the pit at 1800 and analyzed a core by 1900. Frans and Jack drilled the shot holes, laid out the geophone lines, made the shots, and recorded the results on the seismograph. Pleased, they determined that the ice thickness at this location was 3,116.1 m (10,223.4 ft.). Analyzing the previous seismic and gravity data, they found it was almost identical to the profile of the south leg of the traverse from the head of the Skelton Glacier to Apex Depot. The only difference was that the profile of the subglacial topography on this, the north leg, was at a considerably lower elevation. The vast subglacial lowland, now known as the Wilkes Subglacial Basin, sloped from inland to the coast (Appendix A). That evening, with the six-month sun setting lower each week in the southern sky, Jack and Frans described this new find to the team assembled around the dinner table. Recognizing the significance of this discovery made clear the success of the VLT team. Once again, the VLT was proving to be a major source of scientific knowledge and a contributor to polar exploration. The team members could be justly proud.

On Friday, January 15, Frans radioed NAF McMurdo, confirming that Detector and its sled would be abandoned, and the traverse would strive to reach the mountains with the remaining SnoCats and sleds. Dismantling Detector and unloading its useful cargo began in earnest. Detector was stripped, and the parts, tools, other hardware, and provisions were repacked and then reloaded onto Seismo, Mess Cat, and their sleds. Although the temperature was −36 °C (−32.8 °F) at 0600 that morning, it warmed up later in the day, improving working conditions. At 0100, the sun was much lower in the sky than it had been at any time during the traverse. In February, it would descend below the horizon bringing the six-month Antarctic night until the new austral spring arrived next September. The slowly setting sun brought more urgency to getting to the mountains—or radioing for evacuation.

Figure 10.1. Claude is in a good mood. His work is going well.

Figure 10.2. Last view of Detector and its sled as Seismo and Mess Cat headed east. Detector, broken and no longer capable of travel, was abandoned in Victoria Land, and is now well beneath the snow. A radar reflector was left mounted on the sled in the event others might attempt to find them.

The VLT team left this major station at 1530, abandoning Detector on the high plateau (Fig. 10.2) at 148°12′E, 72°07.6′S. Conditions were now cramped when traveling. Jack, Claude, Arnie, and Lou traveled in Seismo, while Bill, Tommy, Al, and Frans traveled in Mess Cat. The VLT team made 11 km (7 miles) that day. At 2230, the temperature was –25 °C (–13 °F); the skies were clear and sunny. Deprived of their usual sleeping quarters (Fig. 10.3), Arnie and Al would sleep in survival tents for the duration of the traverse (Fig. 10.4). They placed their sleeping bags on cots inside the tents, the cots resting on plywood to prevent them from sinking into the snow.

Saturday, January 16, was clear and sunny, with 10 knot (12 mph) winds, and a temperature of –29 °C (–20.2 °F). Before setting out that morning, Tommy replaced the left-rear spring on Mess Cat. At 1300, Seismo stripped teeth from the ring gear in its differential. The rear end needed to be replaced. Seismo had also broken its right-rear spring. After Tommy replaced it, the VLT team traveled for an hour until Seismo suffered a broken front universal joint on the rear drive shaft. Once that was replaced, the SnoCats, Rolligon, and sleds passed through another large depression in the surface. The depression, trough-like, trended 140–150 degrees true. Frans and Jack discussed again how this ice-surface topography related to the ice surface and discoveries

Figure 10.3. Claude, Frans, Arnie, Tommy, Al, and Lou. Arnie and Al were sleeping in survival tents, shielded by the SnoCats.

Figure 10.4. Bill, lamenting the abandonment of Detector Cat.

to the west, the bowl and trough-shaped ice-surface depressions, and the subglacial rock topography.

At 1800 the SnoCats stopped for the day. The engines of both SnoCats had started to miss, and Tommy was again doing his best, but so far without success. Claude mistakenly made a bad gravity reading, and then, adding insult to injury, he hit his head on the gravimeter tripod. At 2315, the temperature was –25 °C (–13 °F) with a 10 knot (12 mph) wind; the skies were clear and sunny with a few clouds to the east. With constant winds, the team was grateful for Explorers' Club (Fig. 10.5)! On the evening's radio schedule, NAF McMurdo asked Frans to send weather observations at 2400 and 1200 for the C-130s that were making flights to the South Pole station. While staying up until midnight held little appeal for Frans, he nonetheless obliged.

Sunday, January 17, was clear and sunny, with an 8 knot (9 mph) wind, and a temperature of –27 °C (–16.6 °F). At breakfast, there was some joking and predicting about how many breakdowns Seismo would have that day. Al even suggested that there be a pool for the number and the kinds of breakdowns. That day, the surface changed—it was comparatively smooth with only small sastrugi. The traverse traveled in third gear, making 37 km (21 miles). The improved surface resulted in substantially fewer breakdowns, except that the cable holding the towing tongue on Mess Cat ruptured. The team, especially Claude, was in a good mood that evening. At 2245, the temperature was –25 °C (–13 °F), with no wind and sparse clouds in the distance.

On Monday, January 18, it was sunny, with clouds on the horizon. There was a 5 knot (6 mph) wind and a temperature of –28 °C (–18.4 °F). At breakfast, Tommy did most of the talking. The topic was equipment breakdowns. Once finished, Tommy

Figure 10.5. Al, making good use of Explorers' Club. His survival tent is to the left. The white banana sled is in front and to the right of the outhouse.

changed a pontoon bearing on Mess Cat. Seismo left first. When Mess Cat was prepared to follow, its engine again failed to start; the batteries were too weak. But after a 15 min wait, Tommy got the engine going. Mess Cat took off an hour after Seismo left. Al, driving in third gear, got bogged down, stalling Mess Cat's engine. Fortunately he managed to restart the engine, and Mess Cat continued to follow Seismo's track. After a long day's travel, Seismo stopped at 1700, and Mess Cat at 1830 at 151°17′E, 72°11′S. Al and Arnie dug 2 m (6.6 ft.) of their pit, finishing by 2200. Frans and Jack prepared the drill holes, geophone lines, and explosives for seismic shots the next day. The weather in the afternoon and evening was very pleasant—no wind and, importantly, no more breakdowns today! The traverse team had made 21 miles over a relatively good surface. At 2150, it was bright and sunny with no wind. The team milled about outside, talking. The temperature seemed warm at –25 °C (–13 °F).

Tuesday, January 19, was also sunny with a few sparse clouds and a 5–8 knot (6–9 mph) wind. The temperature was –23 °C (–9.4 °F). Tommy was the last up at 1115 that morning, and then he installed a new voltage regulator in Mess Cat. Al and Arnie finished digging their pit by 1715. Jack and Frans drilled further and retrieved ice cores, and then they finished their seismic shots by 1600. Their results showed the ice thickness to be 2,716 m (8,909 ft.), where the traverse now neared the mountains. The results confirmed the trough shape of the discovery, the Wilkes Subglacial Basin. Al had trouble sleeping, he said, because of the cold. The temperature had dropped to –30 °C (–22 °F) during the night. The radio schedule with NAF McMurdo was at 2200 with another schedule for the weather report at 2400.

Wednesday, January 20, the temperature was –30.5 °C (–22.9 °F), with a 10–13 knot (12–15 mph) wind, which increased later in the day to 28–35 knots (32–40 mph) with dense blowing snow, 9–15 m (30–50 ft.) high above the surface. Bill asked Frans if he was going to call for a recon before we got too close to the mountains. Frans said, "No, the people at McMurdo know what they're doing." Tommy was again unable to start Mess Cat's engine, but he managed to get it going with a tow from Seismo. The traverse made 38 km (23.5 miles) that day, traveling at 6 kph (4 mph), much faster than on high dense sastrugi. Although the surface remained fairly good, Seismo broke a U-joint on its front drive shaft. With no more spares, Tommy installed two old bearings in the crosses of the U-joint, a temporary but hopefully lasting fix.

On Thursday, January 21, the temperature was –20 °C (–4.0 °F) with winds of 28–30 knots (32–44 mph). Heavy snow had fallen around the vehicles and sleds. We were concerned about Al and Arnie because the tents sometimes were drifted over by snow (Fig. 10.6), preventing them from getting out, and threatening suffocation. Jack and Tommy dug Arnie out of his tent, and Arnie then dug out Al (Fig. 10.7). Both were okay. The weather had deteriorated reducing visibility, the winds buffeting the vehicles and sleds. It was unwise to travel, and therefore a good opportunity to review and consolidate notes and observations. In Seismo, Jack and Frans went over their seismic and

gravity data in ever greater detail, confirming their discoveries. In Mess Cat, Al and Arnie did the same with their snow temperature, density, and ice stratigraphic data, while Claude organized his isotopic notes. Tommy inspected again the vehicles and sleds, while Bill and Lou read and dozed between meals. No sun shots were possible. Frans' music was on all afternoon and evening in Mess Cat. The atmosphere was somewhat surreal, with the sound of Wagner (Frans' favorite) in the polar wind. Frans was content. With the heater on in Mess Cat both afternoon and evening—fuel was now less of a problem—it was cozy and warm, yet somehow unreal. By afternoon, the wind abated, the sky began to clear, and the snow diminished.

On Friday, January 22, the temperature rose to –10 °C (+14 °F), the warmest we'd experienced since the beginning of the journey, with sunshine overhead and scattered clouds on the horizon. But by 1600, heavy cloud cover would move in with light snow. During the noon radio schedule with NAF McMurdo, the VLT team was advised that a P2V would do a recon and spare parts airdrop as soon as weather permitted. They would then fly south to scout for a pass for the traverse through the mountains. If one couldn't be found, or none were passable, they would fly north in an attempt to locate a suitable surface for the landing of an R4D for the VLT team's evacuation. The traverse made 4 km (25.5 miles) that day over an improving surface, stopping at 1730. Al and Arnie finished digging 2 m (6.6 ft.) of the pit in a little over an hour. Frans and Jack drilled for their seismic shots and came in exhausted. The work really wore them out. The past two stations, however, had given good seismic reflection data. The radio contact with Scott Base in the evening revealed that the base had been experiencing bad weather and accumulating snow. The USS *Arneb* left New Zealand the previous night, scheduled to arrive at NAF McMurdo the last part of the month. After dinner, the team shot marbles, two steel ball bearings, on the mess table for a while. After the others left, Tommy, Claude, and Jack played craps with a pair of dice, using matches for money.

On Saturday, January 23, the sky was clear and sunny, with a 10 knot (12 mph) wind and a temperature of –25 °C (–13 °F). That day marked our arrival at our sixteenth major station, Station 548. Everyone was in good humor at breakfast. Lou thought he had spotted mountains yesterday, but they turned out to be clouds because they were gone this morning. We'd been on traverse 100 days as of that day. There were few days left before winter. Al and Arnie finished their glaciological pit, and Jack and Frans completed their seismic work, as at 1945, a Skua gull flew overhead. The ice cores recovered by Frans and Jack were used by Claude for his isotopic analyses, and they were examined by Al and Arnie for glaciology. Radio New Zealand news reported that C-130s were en route to NAF McMurdo. At 2230, there was a 12 knot (14 mph) wind, and the temperature was still –25 °C (–13 °F).

On Sunday, January 24, it was clear overhead with snow blowing 40–50 feet high in a wind of 26 knots (30 mph) and a temperature of –26 °C (–14.8 °F). Static from the blowing snow made the radios all but useless. Because there was no radio

Figure 10.6. Tents buried in a snow drift.

Figure 10.7. Al, having just gotten out of his tent, which had been buried in a snow drift.

communication between vehicles, Frans suggested we leapfrog our travel that day. Seismo would drive for one hour, read instruments, then Mess Cat would move up to Seismo's location, and Seismo would travel ahead for another hour, read its instruments again, and so on throughout the day. Done as a safety measure, Seismo and Mess Cat would therefore stay in closer visual contact. In spite of this less efficient technique, the traverse made 21 km (13 miles). The surface was fairly good. The plane failed to arrive that day. After supper, the wind was still blowing 29–30 knots (33–34 mph). Bill said he found himself sitting and staring off into space for long periods of time, not thinking of anything nor hearing any sounds, although he knew the team was nearby. This was again, the famous *fifty-foot-stare-in-a-ten-foot-room*. Bill thought it was relaxing.

On Tuesday, January 26, the temperature was –30 °C (–22 °F), and the sky was clear and sunny. A 25–28 knot (29–32 mph) wind blew snow 30–40 feet high. The temperature warmed later to –24 °C (–11.2 °F). Mess Cat's engine quit after Seismo left. Seismo returned to assist, but by then Mess Cat had gotten started. A short time later Seismo's fuel line iced up and it took half an hour to clear the ice out of the filter. Jack brought the news that on the previous night's radio schedule, NAF McMurdo reported that a P2V would depart at 1000 today for our location. Claude was happy and singing. We were all in good spirits after hearing this news. Frans suggested that Arnie ride in Seismo that day so that he would be able to ride in Mess Cat to listen for the P2V's arrival. At 1415, Mess Cat broke the front U-joint on its rear drive shaft. Tommy jury-rigged an old drive shaft. The weather deteriorated, and the P2V was unable to fly through heavy snow blowing in at 28–30 knots (32–34 mph), although the sky overhead was clear.

Most of the day the tracks left by Seismo filled in fast; so they were almost impossible for Mess Cat to follow. It was prudent, therefore, after the first stop, for Seismo to travel only half an hour ahead instead of an hour before Mess Cat moved ahead. The traverse made 43 km (27 miles), and then established the seventeenth major station, Station 553. Stopping for the day at 1845, by 1945, Al and Arnie had dug 2 m (6.6 ft.) of their pit and taken the densities and temperatures. Jack and Frans prepared for the next day's seismic shot. In the late afternoon, clouds moved in from the east, clearing by 2200, but by 2300, more clouds were overhead and a whiteout descended. The temperature was −25 °C (−13 °F) with a 12–15 knot (14–17 mph) wind. Mess Cat's heater was out, and a new part was needed. Before dinner, Al, Jack, Frans, and Bill drank martinis. The evening's radio schedule revealed that the P2V was in for maintenance and would be delayed for several days. Claude learned from the message about the Algerian crisis,[1] so he was quite concerned, as he would need to satisfy his military duty once he returned to France. Claude contacted Dumont d'Urville station for more information. After dinner, Jack, Claude, Al, Tommy, and Bill sat in Mess Cat for about an hour talking. Arnie went to his tent, and Lou went to Seismo. Frans was keeping a 2200 radio schedule with NAF McMurdo.

Wednesday, January 27, was hazy with blowing snow; the wind was 20–22 knots (23–25 mph), and the temperature was −24 °C (−11.2 °F). It was noted that the VLT team had been out 104 days, longer than Crary's traverse the previous year. A New Zealand dog team was out 126 days two years prior to our expedition, something of a record. Shortly before dinner, Tommy moved Mess Cat to tighten the tracks—and the fan belt broke. The spare parts box was found to have a large selection of fan belts, but none were the right size. Tommy jury-rigged a belt intended for the hydraulic pump and fitted it on the pulleys. During dinner, the engine overheated as the belt slipped and stretched. Because each SnoCat had a double pulley and two belts, one belt was taken off Seismo and fitted to Mess Cat. We would travel the next day as far as the belts would take us. Frans succeeded in making a temporary fix for the heater in Mess Cat, although it had been seldom used because of fuel conservation needs.

On Thursday, January 28, the weather was bad all day with a whiteout, blowing snow, clouds, and a 15–20 knot (17–23 mph) wind. The temperature was −18 °C (−0.4 °F). It was necessary to lean out of Mess Cat's window when driving to see the tracks left by Seismo. This made the fifth day in a row of bad weather (Fig. 10.8). It seemed unlikely the team would get a recon and resupply flight before reaching the mountains—if it should get that far. A recon would be welcome, because we were still unsure if the traverse had gotten beyond the crevasses reported by the P2V.

From ~1700 on, it was not possible to see the sun. Mess Cat's fuel line iced up five times. With no alcohol left to de-ice the fuel tanks, Seismo's tank iced up three times. The best estimate was that we were now 96 km (60 miles) from the mountains, three

[1]A weeklong insurrection began in Algiers on January 24. Algeria would gain independence from France in 1962.

or four days' travel. Jack was very keen on doing geologic fieldwork in the mountains, although Arnie and Claude had cooled to that idea. There was considerable discussion of how close the VLT team should get to the mountains without a recon. Arnie, Al, Tommy, Lou, and Bill were strongly opposed to getting closer than ~48 km (30 miles). Getting close to the mountains in bad weather would make it difficult to see the surface and any indication of crevassing. Tommy made it very clear that he did not want to go in too close for fear of crevasses. Frans and Jack were in favor of going ahead. Jack acknowledged it would be good to have a recon, but he was unwilling to wait for one. No decision was made. Bill experienced stomach cramping during dinner, which he attributed to the rough ride. At 2210, the temperature was −19 °C (−2.2 °F), with blowing snow, clouds, whiteout, and signs of darkening conditions. Despite the bad weather, the traverse made 33 km (20.5 miles) that day.

Friday, January 29, was cloudy with a whiteout. The wind was 15–18 knots (17–20 mph), and the temperature was −17 °C (+1.4 °F). Frans overslept that morning, and Lou had to wake him. Jack had been concerned for the past few days and wanted to get to the mountains. Before breakfast, Lou groaned about this being yet another day on the "homicide patrol." Now in the vicinity of the mountains, but with no knowledge of the locations of the crevasse fields reported by the P2V, there was understandable concern. Nevertheless, now there was a sense of at least seeing the mountains. We wondered aloud if the "impossible" journey might in fact become a "possible" journey, if we pressed on hard enough. Tommy climbed into Mess Cat somewhat in disbelief, "The visibility is the same as yesterday, but we're going on?" Our experience on the Skelton Glacier and the New Zealand team's accident made the team's concern all the more understandable. Claude (Fig. 10.9) thought we should not go beyond the next major station, if the weather stayed as it was, and if we had no recon. Frans and Jack thought we should carry on, that we would make it. Lou announced that he was going to ride outside the 'Cat on the sled—beginning 56 km (35 miles) from the mountains in order to jump, if crevasses should be encountered.

Seismo burned out the points in its distributor. It took Tommy an hour to fix. Travel stopped at 1830 because the sun had disappeared, although we made 22 km (14 miles) despite the severe whiteout and blowing snow. When driving Mess Cat, it was difficult again to see Seismo's tracks. This made the sixth day of snow or blowing snow, clouds, and whiteout. At 2145, the temperature was −17 °C (+1.4 °F), with 18–20 knot (20–23 mph) winds, snow, and whiteout. Jack, Arnie, and Bill discussed alternatives should the weather not improve. One thought was to request a recon of the weather if not of the crevassed surface. If clear to the north or south, it might be possible to drive out of it. Another thought was that a plane be put on standby at NAF McMurdo, and at the first break in the weather, the VLT team could scout for a landing zone. Yet another thought was to attempt to guide a plane to an instrument landing. None of these ideas was workable, and we knew it. Nonetheless it relieved the tension and uncertainty. Mountaineer that he was, Arnie talked

Figure 10.8. The weather continued to deteriorate.

about walking out to Hallet Station, 320 km (200 miles) away. His idea was not well received. Using both SnoCats, we had enough fuel for 432 km (270 miles). On our evening radio schedule with Scott Base, we learned that the USS *Arneb* had arrived at NAF McMurdo.

On Saturday, January 30, Jack arose early in anticipation of catching first sight of the mountains. The sky had cleared above the snow horizon in the east. There, seeming small and unimposing, a peak appeared! It was the top of a mountain! The VLT team had reached the Transantarctic Mountains! Jack quickly raised the others. At 0800, the clear blue sky revealed the peak to be a large, flat-topped mountain. The team danced, sang, and took

photos of the mountain before breakfast. The good weather and arrival at the mountain sent spirits soaring (Fig. 10.10). For now, the peak was named *Mount Flat Top* (Fig. 10.11). The temperature was a warm −14 °C (+6.8 °F).

At breakfast, conversation was animated. Everyone was happy. Frans radioed Scott Base with the news that mountains had been discovered, and asked them to relay the information to George Toney (USARP representative) at NAF McMurdo, and to tell him also that the weather was good for a recon flight. Unfortunately, the good weather proved to be short-lived. At 1045, as the vehicles started traveling, clouds on the horizon moved in. Mount Flat Top disappeared. By 1100, it was

Figure 10.9. Lou, Claude, Al and Tommy reflect on the dangers that lay ahead. Note that Christmas decorations still adorn the ceiling of Mess Cat.

Figure 10.10. The team was elated at having discovered the Outback Nunataks and the USARP Mountains, and having achieved the long sought Transantarctic Mountains.

whiteout, snowing again, and as bad as the previous day. At 1315, the temperature was −11 °C (+12.2 °F), and the wind was at 15–20 knots (17–23 mph). The traverse stopped at 1300, and the team began putting in the eighteenth major station. The weather continued to deteriorate, with snow and 20 knot (23 mph) wind, whiteout, and visibility ~15 m (50 ft.). Al and Arnie finished digging 2 m (6.6 ft.) by 1400. They did stratigraphy photos of the first meter by 1630 and then stopped for dinner. Frans and Jack drilled again manually and then set up their seismic system. The surface snow was new, very light, one foot deep, and fluffy. Evening dinner was at 1700. The team would finish this station sometime the following day. The big question remained: "How much farther do we travel?"

On Sunday, January 31, the weather was overcast; the visibility was 10–15 miles with a light wind. The temperature was warm at −15 °C (+5 °F). There was a discussion about dirty eating utensils, with Arnie taking some criticism about personal cleanliness. Arnie and Al finished that day's pit around 1545. The results were poor—too much hoar frost. In the afternoon, the clouds lifted, and it was possible to see six mountains. Jack and Al laid out an 800 m (2,624-ft.) baseline for Lou to triangulate the nearest group of nunataks (Appendix H). These would later

Figure 10.11. Mount Flat Top, later to be named Mount Weihaupt by the Advisory Committee on Antarctic Names.

be named the *Outback Nunataks* by the Advisory Committee on Antarctic Names (US-ACAN), discovered by the U.S. Victoria Land Traverse.

It was now apparent to NAF McMurdo, as it had long been apparent to the VLT team, that we would not reach the Tucker Glacier. We would not reach the Ross Sea—the intervening mountains were too formidable. We would not be helicopter lifted to a waiting icebreaker. We were too far away, and there were no suitable passages from the Outback Nunataks to the sea. At our 1200 radio schedule with NAF McMurdo, the VLT team was advised that a schedule had been approved to evacuate us on February 10, or as soon thereafter as weather permitted. The team was to go into the mountains, do whatever scientific work could be accomplished, and make whatever geological and geographical observations the circumstances permitted. If conditions prevented evacuation, the VLT team was to head south toward NAF McMurdo to shorten the distance the plane would need to fly. The message read as follows: "Because of poor weather conditions this season, uncertainty of the time for pickup, and other late season flight commitments, VX6 pickup for you scheduled for 10 Feb., or as soon thereafter as weather permits. Request you work south upon reaching mountains in order to shorten distance from NAF McMurdo to pickup area. Recon and drop will be conducted when weather suitable. Weather between McMurdo Sound and plateau prevented scheduled flight on 30 Jan."

The sun was noticeably lower in the sky each day. Now late in the season, winter was not far off. Claude was in very good humor because he'd picked February 10 and won the pickup date pool. Jack, Claude, and Tommy went through Al Taylor's abandoned gear and picked out things to take back for him. Tommy got Taylor's red vest. If the team was picked up on February 10, the VLT team would have been out 118 days. Al quipped, "This may not be a record, but it's a hell of an average."

After supper, the cloud base had risen, and with no wind, the mountains could be seen clearly. Four mountains were quite visible to the left of the traverse course, another straight ahead, and the top of the large, flat top mountain was now clearly visible. "It's a monster!" exclaimed Bill, and it became something of a visual anchor for the balance of the traverse. Smaller nunataks were distributed all around the vehicles. It now appeared likely that there would be only one or two more travel days. The team agreed to use the time to attempt to enter the mountains. Lou triangulated three small nunataks and found that they were 53 km (33 miles) away. By 2200, the temperature had cooled to −17 °C (+1.4 °F); there was no wind and heavy overcast with visibility at 64 km (40 miles).

On Monday, February 1, the team arose to no wind, high overcast, and a warm day of −19 °C (−2.2 °F). The plane, scheduled to leave NAF McMurdo at 1430 and arrive at our position at 1800, failed to take off. The overcast dissipated, and the sky cleared by noon. The weather now was beautiful, sunny, and with practically no wind; although by 1930, clouds again moved in.

The weather deteriorated, and the nunataks from the previous day turned out to be the tops of nearby mountains. Then the low skies cleared again, and there were many more distant mountains. As we approached the mountains, the vehicles descended 49 m (161 ft.) into a large trough across the trail, then up over several large rollers. Products of the dynamics of massive ice movement, the rollers resulted from the nearness of the mountains and the subglacial topography. From their tops, a broad clear view of the scene ahead appeared.

From the top of an ice ridge, the nearest mountain came clearly into view. An imposing structure, Jack suggested it be called *Mount Welcome,* given the arduous trail that had been taken to discover it. The VLT team parked for the evening on the rise looking toward Mount Welcome, and beyond it a range of mountains extended out of sight both north and south. Estimated to be 6,000–8,000 feet high, they appeared to be the 6,000-foot peaks the P2V had reported some days before. The VLT had, it seemed, made another discovery. These mountains were officially named the *USARP Mountains* (Appendix I) the following year by the US-ACAN. The Committee also named mountains for members of the VLT, viz., for Jack, Al, Claude, and Lou, and for Frans, Bill, Arnie, and Tommy (Appendix F). Each member of the team has expressed his gratitude for this special recognition of the challenges the VLT team overcame, and of the contributions that it made. Jack recommended to the Committee the next year that *Mount Welcome* be named officially, and that a nearby mountain be named *Mount VX-6* in recognition of the support the squadron had provided the VLT team. The Committee did so, also naming the *Outback Nunataks* discovered by the VLT.

The surface was again covered with a foot or more of soft, fluffy snow. After dinner, the team gathered in Seismo for the evening radio schedule with NAF McMurdo. The P2V had not taken off due to bad weather. NAF McMurdo had a 915 m (3,000 ft.) ceiling and 64 km (40 miles) visibility, until local snow showers reduced the visibility to 7 km (5 miles). The flight crew would stand by to come the next day. A C-130 aircraft had taken off from NAF McMurdo, flying to the South Pole Station.

Although the vehicles had to stop to replace Mess Cat's starter, 32 km (20 miles) were made that day, and the team stopped 14 km (9 miles) short of Mount Welcome. At dinner that evening, we talked exclusively about discovery of the Outback Nunataks, Mount Welcome, the USARP Mountains, and the risks that still lay ahead. The team was on the upper reaches of the Rennick Glacier, which had never been seen from the ground prior to this expedition. It was a massive and dynamic glacier, with great waves of ice marking its descent to the Southern Ocean. And it had generated large crevasses. Crevasses took center stage in the team's discussions, raising the question of proceeding over the troughs and rollers farther into the mountains, and of climbing one or more of the peaks. Jack and Frans thought we should attempt another ten or so kilometers, in spite of the rollers due south of us where many open crevasses were visible. The team agreed to go on, but with some reservations.

Chapter 11

First ascent — And near catastrophe

On Tuesday, February 2, the VLT team position was 160°08′E, 72°15′S. There was not much conversation at breakfast, each team member contemplating what had been achieved and what still lay ahead. After breakfast, Seismo moved up 8 km (5 miles) toward Mount Welcome. Mess Cat later followed. When it was within 0.4 km (0.25 miles) of Seismo, Tommy, in Mess Cat, shouted the good news to the others. A VX-6 R4D came into view, circled, and then made a pass (Fig. 11.1). Mess Cat's crew, now with Seismo, rushed out to wave their greetings and watch for the airdrop. A smoke bomb was set off to signal the wind direction, and the R4D adjusted its flight path. The parachute supply long ago exhausted, this was a free-fall drop.

George Toney was on board the R4D. By radio Frans discussed our plans with him. George suggested the traverse head east 56 km (35 miles) into the mountains, then turn south and scout for suitable terrain for an evacuation landing. The landing was still scheduled for February 10, and, if successful, the VLT team would be flown to NAF McMurdo and then shipped

out on the USS *Arneb*. The ship was scheduled to depart NAF McMurdo between February 15 and 20.

The airdrop had been a blessing. In addition to spare parts, which we likely no longer needed, the R4D delivered bread, salami, liverwurst, frozen melon balls, unfrozen beer, paper plates, hot drink cups, mail, and assorted reading material (Fig. 11.2). Given this abundance, the team wondered how long the R4D crew thought the VLT team would continue in the field! Everyone was very excited and jumped out of the 'Cats as the plane made its passes. The mail, which was always the first priority, was quickly opened (Fig. 11.3). Talking stopped then because each of us wanted to learn promptly about family and friends and then digest the news. Mumbles and grunts gave away the summaries of contents, which, by and large, conveyed good news. There was relief—and smiles. Rereading came next and then more smiles and ruminations. The pilot radioed that they could not stay long on station above the VLT as they were heading for the Tucker Glacier to make a recon (Fig. 11.4). The plane

Figure 11.1. The VX-6 makes its free-fall airdrop run.

Figure 11.2. Al, Tommy, Jack, and Claude return with the airdropped packages.

then disappeared into the east as Claude toasted them and bid a fond farewell (Fig. 11.5).

After the last mail reading (Fig. 11.6), everyone retired to Mess Cat, opened the airdropped food and beer, and then talked and shared their good family and friend news, and news of the outer world. A time for fellowship and relaxation, the long-awaited airdrop had happened, and we now had more information, and more direction. Because the plane had headed east to do a recon of the Tucker Glacier, we assumed that meant that we might attempt to make it to the Tucker and traverse down-glacier. The plane returned, however, and after a conversation with Frans,

that option appeared implausible. The situation required further discussion and careful consideration.

The weather turned fine at noon, with sunshine and no wind; so four of the team went outside again to talk about what the VLT team should do. Sitting comfortably once more in soft snow, the feeling was that the team had succeeded in overcoming remarkable and unanticipated challenges to get this far. We had expended enormous effort, and committed all available time and resources to getting to the mountains, which it seemed, had been against all odds. This was not the time to quit. We further talked it over, in earnest tones.

Figure 11.3. Al, Frans, Tommy, Jack, and Claude, sorting through the air-dropped mail.

Figure 11.4. VX-6 (center right) heads for a recon of the Tucker Glacier.

Those at the sit-in-the-snow gathering agreed that the traverse should continue into the mountains later that day and the next day, observe the conditions, consider venturing on foot to one or more of the mountains, if conditions allowed, examine the geology, and collect geological specimens. Jack, Al, Claude, and Arnie (Fig. 11.7) would hike to Mount Welcome, if they could navigate the crevasses, and make a first ascent.

At 1845, Al, Arnie, and Jack left in Seismo to scout closer to Mount Welcome. Jack drove Seismo 6.44 km (four miles) around the south end of the mountain to survey the conditions. The snow surface continued to be soft, .61 m (two ft.) deep with fluffy snow, but with hard snow and ice beneath. From that distance and angle, Mount Welcome appeared to be composed of dark metamorphic rock, intruded by white to light-brown acidic dikes and sills. A moat-like windscoop lay between the glacier

and the mountain's flanks, but the windscoop's depth at this distance could not be determined. We would make the attempt the next day. Lou and Frans, back at camp, made sun shots, while Claude, Tommy, and Bill were in Mess Cat going over the material and supplies that had been air dropped. It was a very pleasant evening at 1915, with the temperature at −10 °C (+14 °F), a 1–2 knot (1–2.3 mph) wind, and light overcast. If all went well, one week from the next day, the team would be evacuated. Until evacuation, our daily routine would be quite different, governed by the surface of the glacier, the nature and number of crevasses, and the peaks now towering above us.

Wednesday, February 3, was warm, −10 °C (+14 °F), but it was cloudy with near whiteout conditions. The visibility was about 90 m (almost a hundred yards). There was a 5 knot (6 mph) wind, and it was snowing. We were unable to travel, given the

Figure 11.5. Claude, toasting the VX-6 flight crew and the long-needed airdrop, as the R4D disappears in the east.

Figure 11.6. Arnie, Claude, Jack, Tommy, and Al reviewed again their mail before more serious discussions about the day or days ahead.

Figure 11.7. Frans, Jack, Bill, Al, and Tommy decided that four of the team should climb Mount Welcome.

uncertain conditions that lay ahead. The snow continued all day, with the wind constructing large drifts of fluffy snow. The team huddled in Seismo or Mess Cat, consolidating notes and getting ready for the approach to Mount Welcome, which would happen the next day. Bill played solitaire for several hours. By 2200, the temperature had cooled to −20 °C (−4 °F).

Thursday, February 4, was another day of greatly reduced visibility, again preventing any thought of going to the mountain. It was a complete whiteout with the temperature at −16 °C (+3.2 °F). Tommy wasn't keen on moving on, but there was still important work that could be done. Jack and Frans still had seismic and gravity observations to make, and Al and Arnie were

anxious to complete another pit or two. Al suggested asking for an extension to February 15 for the evacuation. Jack and Frans agreed, although Tommy and Arnie were less enthusiastic. The team spent the day waiting for improving conditions, reading, and talking while Al, Jack, Claude, and Bill played craps, using playing cards for money. By evening, the whiteout lifted, although it was still heavily overcast (Fig. 11.8). We hoped the weather would allow us to climb the mountain the next day.

On Friday, February 5, the weather was finally good! It was clear and sunny, with a temperature of −20 °C (−4 °F). Jack, Al, Claude, and Arnie left in Seismo at 1045 for Mount Welcome. Frans left at about the same time on skis, headed toward the middle

Figure 11.8. Heavy overcast sky, but with the promise of improving conditions that would allow the first ascent of the mountain.

Figure 11.9. Mount Welcome, exciting and formidable. In the foreground, a sun compass mounted on Seismo beneath the flag which has been diminished by the katabatic winds.

peak from the other side. Lou, Tommy, and Bill stayed with Mess Cat. Lou would triangulate the peaks. When he finished his first observations, he would move to several of his flags set up 1.6 km (a mile) or so away, and he would again shoot those peaks for triangulation. Jack, Al, Claude, and Arnie parked Seismo ~3 km (2 miles) from the southeast spur of Mount Welcome (Fig. 11.9), roped up, and headed for the mountain (Figs. 11.10 and 11.11).

The four of them hiked halfway to the mountain and then paused for a breather. Al and Arnie then took the lead. Closer to the mountain, the snow was .5 m (a foot and a half) deep, making walking difficult. Now in the shadow of Mount Welcome's peak, the mountain loomed above, a stately geologic

giant (Fig. 11.12). Wondering what we'd committed to, we pondered how and where to climb the mountain. We would first find the windscoop and then see what it might offer in getting to the cliffs. We made good progress, heading down a roller to the edge of the windscoop. It ran around the base of the mountain like a moat but without the water. Arnie was first into the windscoop with Al belaying him. Then Jack followed into the windscoop with Claude belaying him.

The windscoop was 23–30 m (75–100 ft.) deep, its blue ice floor sweeping to the mountain's base. The floor was strewn with boulders and smaller rock fragments that had tumbled from the mountain's peaks and slopes. Ahead lay the southeast end

Figure 11.10. Arnie, Claude, and Al get their gear together to climb Mount Welcome. They next roped up with Jack, and headed for the mountain.

Figure 11.11. Jack leads off (not pictured) with Claude following, then Arnie and Al, with Seismo in the background. Hiking to Mount Welcome.

Figure 11.12. Mount Welcome.

of a steep cliff (Fig. 11.13). An ominous cloud moved toward the mountain from the north and east. Jack recorded later that the cliff was composed of metasediments and pegmatite. Above the cliff, a snow and ice ridge was next surmounted (Fig. 11.14), beyond which another much more challenging cliff rose to the left (Fig. 11.15).

Working along the base of the second cliff, the team was surprised to discover semiprecious gems—garnets, glistening from schist and metasediments in the ancient stone wall. The cliff was composed of schistose rocks, which are a common geologic site for garnet. Ice axes proved useful in wedging the garnets from their lair and taking rock samples from the mountain. Jack collected samples,[1] and placed them in small cotton bags. Unable to scale the cliff, the team worked along its base, finding a way up and around it to a snow-covered slope leading to the summit. Claude and Jack worked higher on the mountain (Fig. 11.16), as Al and Arnie, close by, also neared the summit. The Rennick Glacier, sweeping around the mountain (Fig. 11.17), was a massive glacial structure. The first to have set foot on the upper reaches of the Rennick, the VLT team "claimed" it as their own! In the next few days the Rennick would become the highway of the last few days of travel; it would also present unprecedented risk to the survival of the team and traverse.

Then, the weather moved in—Al was the first to spot it. Blowing snow and whiteout next engulfed the mountain, obscuring the south face, and threatening to isolate the party on the peak. In the rising wind, snow could then be seen "water falling" from the summit. Al warned that it was prudent to turn back. The party reluctantly began its descent, rappelling down the steepest

---

[1] In 2005, he donated them to the Byrd Polar Research Center at Ohio State University for their Antarctic archive and library.

Figure 11.13. The first cliff above the windscoop of Mount Welcome. A rope climb enabled the team to get to the cliff top.

Figure 11.14. This ice ridge leads to a snow slope ahead and on the right. Another cliff looms on the left, yet to be surmounted.

Figure 11.15. Arnie, at the top of a snow slope at the base of the second cliff.

Figure 11.16. Claude and Jack stop for a breather, with Jack looking at the summit.

Figure 11.17. View from a cliff nearing the summit of Mount Welcome. Claude is at right below. The blue ice far below and in the background is one of the many great swells in the upper reaches of the Rennick Glacier, first explored by the VLT team.

cliffs, and sliding down snow-covered slopes. Al belayed Arnie, and Claude belayed Jack as they worked their way down the mountain cliffs and snow-covered slopes and into the windscoop at the bottom. The wind continued unabated.

Once out of the windscoop at ~1600, Al found himself in considerable pain during the trek back to Seismo. The muscles in his thighs had been overtaxed. He could walk only very slowly. Lack of exercise from the waist down over the months had its effect on all members of the traverse. The trek from the mountain was difficult for all four of us. The strenuous hike seemed like it took hours! The party's tracks made earlier from the SnoCat to the mountain had long since been erased. Though the clouds had largely dissipated and the wind on the glacier had abated, the deep snow proved almost unsurpassable. Jack was in the lead, with Claude at the other end of his rope, and Arnie, roped to Al, followed, bringing up the rear. The deep snow required that feet be lifted high to make each step, straining both legs and groins. Exhausted well before reaching the vehicle, twenty paces was the maximum that could be managed before stopping for resuscitation and recovery of the legs and groins. Breaths came in gulps.

During the agonizing struggle, Al finally gave up some distance from Seismo. Arnie walked out to tell Claude and Jack that Al couldn't make it (Fig. 11.18). Claude, Jack, and Arnie trekked back to recover Al and help him the rest of the way to Seismo. Seismo returned to camp at 1810. Mess Cat was at the end of a base line with Lou triangulating more peaks, so it joined Seismo at 1930. It had been a strenuous but satisfying day.

At the 1945 radio schedule with Scott Base, George Toney advised the VLT team that a possible evacuation had been rescheduled for February 8, due to an emergency flight needed to evacuate an American meteorologist from Ellsworth Station. The

American had been scheduled for evacuation by an Argentine ship, which was now in danger of being stranded in the offshore ice for another year, if it attempted his rescue. At 2300, the temperature was −27 °C (−16.6 °F) and clear, with a 5 knot (6 mph) wind. The sun, now not far above the horizon from dawn to dusk, was setting in the south and west over the Victoria Land Plateau (Fig. 11.19), a reminder of the lateness of the season, and of the challenges yet ahead. The VLT team had dinner at 2130.

On Saturday, February 6, up early, the traverse headed east and then south up the Rennick Glacier, which had not been traversed previously (Fig. 11.20). It was clear and sunny with a light wind and a cloud front moving in from the north. The temperature was −24 °C (−11.2 °F). The traverse made good time over a good surface of soft deep snow that thinned as the SnoCats and sleds descended 41 m (135 ft.) to the bottom of a blue ice valley. The team soon found itself traveling over more huge rollers, the SnoCats straining up the steep sides and careening down the far sides. The heavy sleds pushed the SnoCats (which had no brakes) down the steep side of the rollers. As the SnoCats traveled down the rollers, the sleds tended to slide to one side or the other. The SnoCats rolled and slid almost uncontrollably, threatening to jackknife all the way. It took considerable driving skill and effort to avoid vehicle and sled jackknifing. The roof hatches were opened on both Seismo and Mess Cat. Jack would peer out from the top of Seismo and guide Frans, who was at the wheel. Behind, while Al drove, Bill did the same from the top of Mess Cat, scanning ahead for signs of trouble.

From the bottom of an ice valley, heading now up-glacier, yet another ice ridge loomed, this one the tallest and steepest we had seen. With the view up-glacier obstructed by the ridge, Seismo and Mess Cat climbed laboriously to the summit, with engines

Figure 11.18. Arnie, returning to report that Al needed help. Claude, heading back to find Al.

Figure 11.19. The six-month sun sets low over the Victoria Land horizon as shadows lengthen. The six-month winter is on its way.

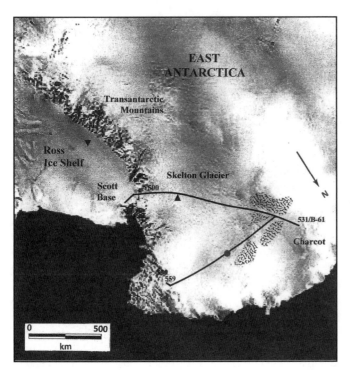

Figure 11.20. The Victoria Land Traverse team had met its goal. It now was in the mountains!

roaring. At the ridge top, Seismo, with no brakes, began its roll down the other side. Still straining at the wheel, Frans was fixed on the scene ahead until—Jack sounded the alarm—"crevasses on your left!" The largest crevasses we had seen since leaving Scott Base loomed a hundred meters (328.1 ft.) from the 'Cat (Fig. 11.21). Frans held steady to the wheel, scanning ahead for

more crevasses as the SnoCat and sled now careened full speed past the yawning chasm, threatening to jackknife and overturn, but slid mercifully into the ice valley bottom. Mess Cat, now topping the ridge and unsuspecting, with Al at the wheel, began its downward plunge. Al, struggling with the same view that Frans had, and Bill peering from the hatch, Mess Cat raced down the icy slope, weaving from side to side, threatening to overturn, and then it slid to a peaceful roll alongside Seismo!

Miraculously, the SnoCats and sleds did not overturn. Amazingly, the SnoCats and sleds held together. Looking back, three huge open crevasses lay brief yards from our course. Astonishingly, the SnoCats and sleds did not careen to the bottoms of the yawning crevasses! Had the vehicles been slightly farther to the east, Seismo and Mess Cat would have disappeared forever! The U.S. Victoria Land Traverse would have vanished, and, almost surely, no search would ever have revealed their final destination. That we missed the crevasses was pure luck. The "ice angels were at our side," proclaimed Jack at dinner. The team all sighed and nodded. A solemn moment followed.

The SnoCats changed course three times during the rest of the day, avoiding ice ridges, valleys, and crevasses as best they could. The VLT team made 60 km (37.5 miles), one of the best daily distances traveled during the entire traverse. Making the final station farther up the glacier amid the Outback Nunataks and within the USARP Mountain Range, they stopped the Sno-Cats at 2000, at Station 559, to be abandoned there forever. Al and Arnie dug their last pit, as Frans and Jack drilled their last ice hole, and laid their final geophone spread. They would make the shot the next day.

In just four months, the Victoria Land Traverse team had covered the 2,400 km that had been set for them (Appendix J). It was not known at the time of planning, or even when the VLT team

Figure 11.21. The crevasses as the VLT team proceeded up-glacier on the Rennick. **A** represents the view Jack and Frans had as they approached the ice ridge summit, and that Bill and Al had soon after. **B** is the view that revealed itself as the SnoCats topped the ridge and careened down the south slope of the other side. The USARP Mountains are in the background.

left Scott Base, that the journey might well have been impossible. Nonetheless, with the cooperation from NAF McMurdo, the critically important VX-6 and C-124 airdrops, and the strength and determination of the VLT team, the scientific and historic undertaking was a success. The "impossible" was, as fate would have it, "possible." The final route of the VLT (Appendix J), seismic data (Appendix K), glaciological data (Appendix L), and the traverse stations, locations and elevations (Appendix M) have been reduced and archived at the VLT teams' universities and institutions. Discoveries included the Wilkes Subglacial Basin, the Wilkes Land Anomaly, the region of chaotic ice, the anomalously great continental ice sheet thickness, the anomalous complex subglacial topography, the Outback Nunataks, the upper reaches of the Rennick Glacier, and the USARP Mountains. Seemingly against all odds, and without loss of life, the impossible journey was completed.

On the radio schedule with NAF McMurdo, it was learned that evacuation was growing problematic. The weather and the forecast were not looking favorable, and the sastrugi surface on the glacier looked foreboding. The men of VX-6 Squadron had done a remarkable job, but, and we could hardly disagree, the chances of safe landing were diminishing. And, of course, there was, at that point in time, no way the VLT team could make it to the Ross Sea via the Tucker Glacier or any other avenue. If the evacuation attempt should be made, the traverse team would need to locate a suitable sastrugi-free zone that was long enough for safe landing and safe takeoff. The odds were seemingly against the team. The sun was setting ever lower in the west (Fig. 11.22). That evening at dinner, the group discussed and contemplated the future.

What no one knew was that plans were being made to abandon the VLT, its vehicles, sleds, and personnel for the six-month winter. With the season waning, the weather uncooperative, and the high sastrugi ever present, the options for rescue were diminishing. The new plan, the team later learned, was for VX-6 to airdrop a ten- by twenty-foot insulated, ribbed, canvas-covered Jamesway U.S. Army hut. This would be the team's home for the six-month winter. Airdropped with the Jamesway would be provisions for the long duration, and fuel for a heater. The VLT team would hunker down until the austral spring next September and then hope for its evacuation.

Figure 11.22. The Antarctic winter prowling below Victoria Land's horizon; the southern sun would shortly disappear.

Chapter 12

⊷⊶ ⊷⊶

Rescue and reprieve

Sunday, February 7, was greeted with strong winds of 35–40 knots (40–46 mph), sun, a clear daytime sky, blowing snow, and a temperature of −20 °C (−4 °F). The snow was drifting heavily, so much so that Al and Arnie couldn't work in the pit. Frans and Jack were struggling with their geophone lines, while the blowing snow and background noise were making seismic recording impossible. After breakfast, Mess Cat drove back along the inbound track to tie in the altimetry. Once Mess Cat returned, believing that this station was the end of the traverse, several of the team stayed in Mess Cat relaxing, reading, and talking. Lou worked up his sun shot data, and because of the blowing wind and snow preventing seismic work, Frans snoozed in Seismo, and Jack worked on the gravity data. Claude cooked the evening meal of spaghetti, roast beef, ice cream, and strawberries, all from the airdrop. The radio schedule with Scott Base revealed again that there was no news about evacuation. At 2215, the temperature was −25 °C (−13 °F) with a 23 knot (26 mph) wind; the skies were clear with blowing snow and the sun was disappearing in the west. Except for a brief trip for the refraction shot, the 'Cats had travelled their last mile. The VLT team was to remain at the station in this ice valley until further notice.

On Monday, February 8, the team got up at 0845. The temperature was the same as the previous day. Al and Arnie found that their pit was badly drifted over. They spent considerable time clearing it out so that they could proceed with their observations. Their work was finished by 1430. Frans and Jack finished their seismic refraction shot in spite of the 20–25 knot (23–29 mph) blowing wind. At the noon radio schedule, NAF McMurdo requested another weather report at 1800, informing the team that VX-6 was considering a landing the next day, if the sastrugi was manageable. Frans was advised to scout the area for a suitable landing zone, to prepare for such a landing, and to have the equipment and personnel ready to be loaded on an aircraft. While pleased with the message, and while the VLT had found a comparatively smooth low sastrugi surface nearby on the glacier, the team was accustomed to disappointment. The news was greeted with reservation. Nevertheless, obliged to prepare for evacuation, everyone set to work, spending the balance of the day packing up the gear that might be taken out. Bill made an inventory of food to be left as a cache for later explorers, should our evacuation be successful. Jack and Frans packed up the seismic, gravity, and magnetic gear, and their abundant data and seismic records. Al and Arnie collected their glaciological data, as Tommy donned his best unsoiled gear. Claude secured his snow samples for isotopic analysis and tucked them securely in his duffle bag (Fig. 12.1). From these data, a variety of important papers would be published (Appendix N). Al secured Explorers' Club for possible evacuation. A historical icon, it was hoped there would be room for it on the R4D. Tommy decided not to waste the dwindling libations (Fig. 12.2). Seismo was detached from its sled and parked clear of what might be the landing zone. The same was done for Mess Cat, with the Rolligon and sled both removed and parked behind Seismo. In the evening, the wind was still blowing hard at 25 knots (29 mph). Some clouds were moving in from the west and north. There was limited confidence in the next day's scheduled evacuation.

Tuesday, February 9, was sunny with scattered clouds, a light wind, and −20 °C (−4 °F). At 0800, Frans made radio contact with NAF McMurdo. The plane was on its way! It was scheduled for arrival at 1430, i.e., "Navy R4D, #17219 is in the air and on its way up the Ferrar Glacier en route to the Victoria Land Traverse on the Rennick Glacier." Everyone rolled up his sleeping bag and parked it on the pile of waiting gear. It was in fact a precaution in the event the aircraft had a mishap, or needed to set down due to the heavy load on its return. The team sat in Mess Cat, finished the last of the beer, and listened to the plane's radio report to NAF McMurdo.

Around 0930, low clouds rolled in from the north as the team watched the sky. Twenty minutes before the plane's scheduled arrival, low clouds consumed the glaciers and the mountains. The sides of the valley were no longer visible. The R4D radioed at 1400 saying they were attempting to find the VLT team. The blue sky to the south had disappeared as haze and clouds moved in. Visibility was reduced to zero. Each of the team anxiously watched the clouds and listened for the plane. Amid the scores of mountains, the plane too was at risk. Finally the pilot radioed to say that they had failed to find the VLT team's location. The plane was running low on fuel and was returning to NAF

Figure 12.1. Claude, getting ready for the R4D landing, with his isotopic samples in his duffle bag.

Figure 12.2. Tommy, ensuring that selected valuables would not be left behind. The seismograph, its recorder and related gear, are to the left, ready for evacuation.

McMurdo. They'd try again the next day. It was a letdown! After dinner Bill played solitaire, and Jack started a game of hearts with Al, Tommy, and Claude. Frans and Lou stayed in Seismo. Al relaxed, saying "Well, I have my tent up; so I don't care when they come." Claude said, "We'll read tonight, have a good sleep, and be picked up tomorrow." Frans complained, "The thing that gets to me is not being able to do anything while waiting for the plane. We can't make a refraction shot or go further into the mountains." He then suggested driving to the nearest mountain "to collect rock samples—or something." Two hours after the plane departed, the ceiling lifted. The sky cleared, and the VLT was accessible.

On Wednesday, February 10, everyone arose at 0900. The day was warm, partly cloudy, with almost no wind, and the temperature was −15 °C (+5 °F). The same plane that tried the previous day would make another try. Navy R4D, #17219 was airborne at 0945 and expected to arrive at our position ~1230. It was mostly clear that day. The mountains to the northeast extended out of sight. Frans seemed to be getting religion. When asked if the plane would make it on this day, to everyone's surprise he said, "Yes, God willing!" The plane arrived at 1230, and the VLT team was visible.

Smoke flares were lighted for wind direction. The R4D headed straight toward the camp, descending confidently above the horizon. Everyone was conscious, particularly the flight crew, of the dangers lurking in the wind-worn surface of sastrugi and hard snow. Unseen sastrugi or a host of the icy waves could mean disaster on landing, or on takeoff once the plane was heavily loaded. The R4D touched down expertly in a swirl of snow. A cheer went up! The plane headed for our

Figure 12.3. Al, watching the arrival of "our evacuation."

encampment (Fig. 12.3) as the team anticipated its rescue and reprieve (Fig. 12.4).

The plane made it to the VLT team location. Lieutenant Commander Bob Dale, the pilot, and his crew disembarked from the plane. Handshakes and greetings in the snow made clear our pleasure at seeing them. Good men, we to this day appreciate their support and sacrifice. The VLT team and the airplane crew set about loading gear (Fig. 12.5). The scientific equipment and instrumentation and the scientific notes and data received first priority. Then personal possessions were loaded. Because of the concern about overloading, the rest of the gear remained behind—the unneeded contents of the vehicles and sleds; the vehicles; the Rolligon and sleds; the unused stores of food, tools, explosives, fuel, and spare parts. All of these were cached for future expeditions.

It was a somewhat melancholy moment as the team boarded the R4D. The door was closed. The engines roared. The R4D picked up speed, rumbling across sastrugi, vibrating uncontrollably. Not yet airborne, Bob Dale's copilot fired the JATO bottles, and with the assisted lift sent the R4D airborne with a jolt. The jolt, we learned upon landing back at NAF McMurdo, came when a JATO bottle broke loose, bounced off the sastrugi, and tore a gash in the plane's elevator. In flight, Bob and his copilot experienced difficulty controlling the plane

Figure 12.4. Bill and Arnie, watching anxiously as the R4D approaches.

Figure 12.5. Loading gear. Jack, Arnie, Al, Tommy, and Lou are in front of the plane door.

for reasons they did not understand. It was only upon landing at NAF McMurdo and observing the elevator damage that the reason for the difficult in-flight handling became clear. The VLT team once more was lucky!

Peering from the airplane windows at the time of takeoff, the team was quiet. Seismo and Mess Cat, the Rolligon and sleds were abandoned to harsh Antarctica (Fig. 12.6). They would not be seen again. Today they reside beneath the snow, fossils of our grand adventure. The R4D winged its way north, then, from the USARP Mountains to the coast of the Southern Ocean. The plane circled over the foot of the Rennick Glacier where it debouches into the sea, then headed south along the Transantarctic Mountains. With the plane still flying on the west side of the mountains, the pilot searched for an opening. A valley glacier flowing to the

Ross Sea offered a flight avenue, and the R4D banked east. Over the Ross Sea, the plane approached NAF McMurdo. The USS *Arneb* lay at anchor in the harbor (Fig. 12.7), a short distance offshore from NAF McMurdo, our way back to our distant homes.

At 1900, the plane landed on the ice shelf near Scott Base. There the team deplaned to a waiting VX-6 helicopter that ferried them over Observation Hill to NAF McMurdo. A warm reception from George Toney, VX-6 Squadron personnel, the base commander, and importantly the base cook, awaited the team. The VLT team's attire set them apart from its well-tailored hosts, but no one seemed to notice, or they were too polite to comment. Shown to our new quarters, the day was devoted to discarding clothing, taking showers, enjoying warm food, and answering endless questions. In the showers we found that our skin had

Figure 12.6. Seismo, Mess Cat, Rolligon, and sleds as we left them in a row, marked by trail flags.

Figure 12.7.The USS *Arneb* is in the lower left. NAF McMurdo Station is directly ahead in the middle of the picture, and Observation Hill is to the right.

flaked and peeled off from our bodies. Frans looked at Jack and proclaimed, "Adonis." Jack looked at Frans and said, "Sampson." Manual drilling had made a difference in both physiques and strength. Pit digging had done the same for Al and Arnie. Comfort, rest, and relaxation were now the order of the day. A few of us headed for the beer hall and enjoyed refreshments, while absorbing the scene around us.

In clean clothes, the team went next to the Mess Hall where a wonderful, long-forgotten kind of meal was served. Afterward the team was invited by the commanding officer of NAF McMurdo, Commander Lloyd Bertoglio for drinks, more food, and conversation. The team then retired to its new quarters, each sleeping a long night away. The next day the team was shown new SnoCats (Figs. 12.8 and 12.9) that would be used by its successors. Substantially redesigned, these SnoCats would provide considerably more space and comfort, and, more importantly, they were designed to better withstand the rigors of the trail based upon the VLT team's experience. Tommy was both jealous and delighted! Jack would use them one year later at South Pole Station on a new seismic and gravity survey—this one intended to determine the thickness of the continental ice sheet at the South Pole and profile a section of the South Pole's subglacial topography.

The few days remaining before the VLT team's departure were spent packing scientific data and records for transport to universities and institutes where the data would be analyzed. The scientific instruments that the VLT brought back from the traverse were carefully stored for future use.

Figure 12.8. Jack, inspecting the newly designed, much larger SnoCats to be used in later seasons.

Figure 12.9. Claude, inspecting the interior of the new SnoCats.

Figure 12.10. Port Lyttelton, New Zealand.

Frans, Jack, Bill, Tommy, Lou, and Claude departed February 16 from NAF McMurdo as the sun set on Antarctica, and *our* Victoria Land. We sailed through the "roaring forties" on the USS *Arneb,* arriving in Port Lyttelton, New Zealand, on February 22, 1960 (Fig. 12.10). The *Arneb*, a military troop transport ship, had limited sleeping quarters, so cots were set up for the team in one of the cargo holds, quarters much better and far more spacious than those in Detector, Seismo, and Mess Cat. Al Stuart and Arnie Heine remained behind at Scott Base, where over the next

few weeks they worked with Charles Swithinbank on the Ross Ice Shelf. On March 13, Al and Arnie departed for New Zealand on the last ship from NAF McMurdo that season, the icebreaker *Atka*, arriving in Port Lyttelton on March 22, 1960.

As the USS *Arneb* docked in Port Lyttelton, the Navy VX-6 Lockheed Constellation made a low welcoming pass, a tribute to the VLT team. On the dock, a group of New Zealanders waited to greet the team (Fig. 12.11). One of those waiting was Barbara Cranefield, a friend of Jack's. Another was Mary Pat Gamble,

Figure 12.11. New Zealanders were waiting on the dock to greet the VLT team.

a friend of Bill's. Mary Pat had sent the bottle of scotch that was air-dropped to the VLT team. Some members of the VLT team were given quarters in U.S. Navy housing at the Christchurch airport, while others made their ways to various parts of Christchurch or elsewhere in New Zealand. A few headed for the United States and home.

The Victoria Land Traverse was over. While it has taken some years to reflect on and appreciate the significance of that journey, it was a defining moment in all our lives. Brothers from that high adventure, each of us is grateful to have been chosen for this historic undertaking, to have been given the opportunity to contribute meaningfully to scientific knowledge, and to have survived the challenges. Victoria Land's mountains and its plains remain the sentries for others yet to come.

The late summer sun setting behind Mina Bluff, with the Ross Ice Shelf in the foreground, as it was now setting also in Victoria Land. The VLT team had avoided abandonment. The start of the six-month winter was only days away.

Epilogue

Some forty-two years had passed since the end of the Victoria Land Traverse when the team held its 2002 reunion at Jack's home in Evergreen, Colorado. It was there that we decided to undertake the compilation and writing of this book.

All of the team disbursed after the VLT, each going in his own direction. Frans, Al, Jack, Claude, and Bill returned to graduate programs at their universities where they received their Ph.Ds. Jack, Al, Claude, and Bill became professors at different universities. Jack went to the Geophysical and Polar Research Center, University of Wisconsin–Madison, where he worked on the VLT seismic, gravity, and geologic data he had collected. He married Audrey Reis of Waunakee, Wisconsin, on January 28, 1961. A year later Jack returned to Antarctica to conduct seismic and gravity surveys at the South Pole Station, where, after unsuccessful attempts by British, Russian, and American scientists, he became the first to successfully measure ice thickness at the South Pole (Weihaupt, 1963). After receiving two M.S. degrees, he received his Ph.D. from the University of Wisconsin in 1973.

Jack has held a number of corporate, government, and academic positions including a position as exploration geologist for the Buchans Mining Company in Newfoundland; exploration geologist for the Chile Exploration Company of the Anaconda Company in Chile, South America; seismologist with the United Geophysical Corporation in the continental United States; chairman of the Department of Physical and Biological Sciences for the U.S. Armed Forces Institute in Madison, Wisconsin; associate dean of science at Indiana University in Indianapolis; associate dean of science and assistant dean of the Graduate School for Purdue University in Indianapolis; vice president of the University Foundation, associate vice president for academic affairs, and dean of the Graduate School at San Jose State University, California; and vice chancellor for academic affairs at the University of Colorado Denver. He is emeritus professor of geology at the University of Colorado Denver and resides with his wife in Evergreen, Colorado, where he continues his research and writing.

On the basis of his VLT work, Jack and his colleagues are credited with the discovery of the Wilkes Subglacial Basin in East Antarctica, and the discovery of what may be the largest meteorite impact crater on Earth. This feature is located beneath the continental ice sheet where he and Frans also discovered the Wilkes Land (Gravity) Anomaly. Jack has continued his work on meteorite impact phenomena, on the associated gravity spectrum of Antarctica, and on annual and century-scale variations in the Antarctic continental ice sheet and associated global sea-level variations, utilizing aerial photographs and satellite remote-sensing data. He is credited also with the discovery of the 1531 Orontius Finaeus map, which reveals the Antarctic continent's discovery in the sixteenth century or earlier, in contrast to the 1821 date commonly reported in contemporary history books.

Jack also was a First Lieutenant in the Third Combat Engineer Battalion of the Twenty-Fourth Infantry Division in Korea, commanded 1,000 troops, and was promoted to Battalion Adjutant (a position held by General Douglas MacArthur when he was a junior officer) and Assistant Division Engineer on the general's staff. Jack presently holds a commission as Captain in Naval Intelligence in the U.S. Navy. He is also the great-nephew of George Rogers Clark and his brother Captain William Clark of Northwest Territories fame. Jack is also the recipient of a number of recognitions including military medals and the Madisonian Medal.

Al returned to his hometown in Roanoke, Virginia, and then went to the Byrd Polar Institute, now the Byrd Polar Research Center, at Ohio State University to analyze and write up his Antarctic data. He planned to return to Antarctica the following season, ordering 1,000 bamboo poles to be sent to Antarctica as trail markers and accumulation stakes. He was reacquainted with Mary Louise Moyers, and they were married on December 20, 1960. Bill Smith, who was living in Washington, D.C., at the time, served as a groomsman in Al's wedding. Al and Mary Louise have four children, Sarah Park, Amy, Julia, and Peter. Given his marriage and growing interest in economic and demographic change, Al decided to give up his glaciological work and instead pursue a doctorate at Ohio State in geography. After finishing his course work, he took a planning job in Roanoke, Virginia, where he worked on his dissertation and pursued his interest in the southern United States, which allowed him, nonetheless, to teach classes about the polar world. After earning his Ph.D., Al taught for five years at the University of Tennessee–Knoxville, and then moved to the University of North Carolina at Charlotte in 1969. At UNC–Charlotte he served as chair of the Department of Geography and Earth Sciences for seventeen years. Al retired in 1999 as professor emeritus and lives with his wife in Charlotte, North Carolina.

Frans returned to the Netherlands and in 1964 received his Ph.D. from Delft University of Technology. He went on to be employed by various companies, working in areas throughout the world, such as iron ore mining in Liberia, seismology in Chad, and monitoring underground Soviet nuclear activities for the Lamont-Doherty Earth Observatory, Columbia University. He also worked for the United Nations Educational, Scientific, and Cultural Organization (UNESCO) in Korea after the Korean War, and next worked on the drifting Arctic Ice Island T3, for the University of Washington. Frans continued doing fieldwork for various companies all over the world, including seismic exploration out of Houston, Texas. In 1968, while working for the University of Washington, Frans married Anita, and he and his bride returned to the Netherlands. A number of years later he lost Anita to illness. Frans is retired and spends his time skiing, flying his ultralight aircraft, racing in the Tour de France, riding his BMW motorcycle, taking his dog for walks in the fields of France, and, in conjunction with Jack, doing calculations on cosmic mass and motion, and the age of the universe. Frans lives in his country villa in Besmont in northern France.

Claude returned to France, received his doctorate, and joined the French National Center for Scientific Research (CNRS), later becoming director of that institute. He also served as expedition leader in Adélie Land, Antarctica, and then as a member of the Victoria Land Traverse, experiences that enabled him to formulate current hypotheses of global climate change over past millennia and on contemporary Earth. These efforts eventually led to the recognition of the Anthropocene Era, which began climatically and anthropically with the industrial era. Claude also continued his work in Antarctica, with 22 subsequent expeditions to that continent over a stretch of more than forty years. During that time he was engaged in the Dome Concorde and Vostok campaigns, drilling the East Antarctic continental ice sheet to "age depths" of 40,000 and 150,000 years respectively.

Claude has received many honors and much recognition for his research, and in 2001, at a ceremony in Bern, Switzerland, he was awarded the International Balzan Foundation Balzan Prize for Climatology for his research on ice. His award noted that "Dr. Lorius discovered that the isotopic composition of ice may indicate the temperature at the time of precipitation, and demonstrated that it is possible to determine atmospheric pressure at the time of ice formation from such analyses." The Balzan Foundation noted further that "his data have not only played a crucial role in the reconstruction of climate changes over past millennia, but also helped us understand the close relation between climate and the concentration of greenhouse gas in the atmosphere, and how dependent the atmosphere is on human activities." Claude was also president of French Polar Expeditions, founder of the French Institute for Polar Research, and initiator of the European Project for Ice Coring in Antarctica (EPICA), and he was elected to the French Academy of Sciences in 1994. He is also the recipient of numerous prizes, including the Humboldt Prize, Polaire Belgica Prize, Italgas Prize, Tyler Prize for Environmental Achievement, CNRS Gold Medal, SCAR Medal, and Blue Planet Prize. Claude is retired and lives in his home in the French Alps, close to Grenoble, France.

Bill returned to George Washington University, where he received his Ph.D. He went on to lead a team conducting research on psychotropic medication for the California Department of Mental Health. Following that he was a research scientist with the Walter Reed Army Institute of Research, Division of Neuropsychiatry, carrying out studies in Barrow, Alaska, and Inuvik, Northwest Territories, Canada. In 1970, Bill joined the faculty at the newly established University of Wisconsin campus at Green Bay. In 1978, while on sabbatical, he was a visiting scholar at the Scott Polar Research Institute, Cambridge University, England, and in the mid-1980s he conducted environmental housing studies on kibbutzim in the Negev Desert in Israel. Bill retired as professor emeritus from the University of Wisconsin–Green Bay in 1995. Being a native Californian, Bill returned to the west and now lives in Las Vegas, Nevada, where he enjoys visits from his two sons.

Lou Roberts had graduated from the University of Colorado Denver with a degree in civil engineering before going on the traverse. He was employed by the Topographic Division of the U.S. Geological Survey (USGS) and was on special assignment to the VLT. When the traverse was over, Lou returned to the USGS. During the early 1960s, Lou supervised mapping surveys in Thailand, Laos, and Cambodia, and carried out field surveys in the continental United States and Alaska. Lou was married in 1964 while assigned to USGS Topographic Division Headquarters in Denver, Colorado. In 1976, he was posted to the USGS Topographic Division in Washington, D.C./Reston, Virginia, where he was involved in international mapping and surveying projects, some of which were in Saudi Arabia, Yemen, and Egypt. From 1976 to 1980, Lou remained in Washington, D.C./Reston in the Resource Management Section of the Topographic Division. Lou retired in 1980 and lives in Arvada, Colorado.

After the traverse, Arnie continued working in Antarctica and was appointed field officer with the Antarctic Division in the Department of Scientific and Industrial Research (DSIR) in Wellington, New Zealand. In addition to organizing New Zealand Antarctic field programs, Arnie began the McMurdo Ice Shelf Project, which later was extended to the Lake Vanda area. Arnie got married in 1967. In 1970, he transferred to the Engineering Seismology section of DSIR, and in 1983, he returned to Antarctica as a member of the Erebus Ice Tongue Project, making further visits to *The Ice* as part of the Sea Ice Project until his retirement from DSIR in 1986. Arnie and his wife live in Days Bay on the eastern coast of Wellington Harbor.

Tommy, a U.S. Navy Seabee, joined the VLT team as a replacement for Ray Clem, also a Navy Seabee mechanic, who became ill just before the VLT team left Scott Base. Clem was himself a replacement for an Australian mechanic, John Russell, who became ill after arriving at McMurdo. Tommy was supposed to be with the VLT team for only a week, but ended up completing the entire traverse. He played a critical role maintaining the SnoCats and sleds. The successful completion of the traverse was in large measure due to his knowledge and skill, and his success as a mechanic. He was the youngest member of the team, celebrating his 23rd birthday while on the traverse. Tommy spent six years in the navy, was married in 1962, and lived with his wife, Libby, in Oxnard, California. There he worked for the Caterpillar Tractor Company for nine years, before moving to Bloomfield, New Mexico, where he worked in the oil fields building compressors. His work was highly regarded, and an oil well, the "Baldwin Eagle," was named for him. Tommy passed away December 1, 1992. He is survived by his wife Libby and their daughter.

Al Taylor was employed by the U.S. Geological Survey and was on assignment to the VLT. Thirteen days after the traverse left the head of the Skelton Glacier, Taylor became ill. A helicopter piloted by Lieutenant Commander Edgar A. (Al) Potter and the helicopter crew chief made the very long and dangerous flight from NAF McMurdo to the VLT team location in interior Victoria Land to evacuate Taylor to NAF McMurdo. Taylor then returned to the United States. Over the years, Taylor has been involved in geologic mapping and fuel and mineral resource investigations in several states and abroad. From 1984 through 1987, he was a geological consultant. Since 1988, he has been with the Virginia Department of Mines, Minerals and Energy in their Division of Mineral Resources. Taylor lives with his wife in Virginia.

Navy Chief Petty Officer Warren Jackman, a Navy photographer, was with the traverse from its departure from Scott Base to the head of the Skelton Glacier. He left the VLT at that point and was airlifted back to NAF McMurdo. Warren passed away April 24, 1985.

Soon after the Victoria Land Traverse, the team members were notified by the National Science Foundation that the Advisory Committee on Antarctic Names (US-ACAN) and the U.S. Board on Geographic Names had named mountains for each of the team members: Mount Weihaupt, Mount Van der Hoeven, Mount Stuart, Mount Lorius, Mount Baldwin, Mount Heine,

Roberts Butte, and Smith Bench in the USARP Mountains, the range discovered by the VLT team. In the years that followed, members of the team published a variety of scientific papers (Appendix N), all based ultimately on the data collected while on the Victoria Land Traverse.

Reflecting on the Victoria Land adventure, Frans has shared with members of the team his remembrances of "the enormity, and the danger," that made a lasting imprint on his life. His subsequent adventures, difficult as some were, were nevertheless "nowhere as important and memorable as that of the Victoria Land Traverse in Antarctica." Al, in retrospect, has said, "These polar experiences were some of the most significant of my life. In my early twenties I had become something of an agnostic. However, I came to appreciate God's creativity that was evident in the awesome power and beauty of this frozen world. This experience became something of an epiphany for me, one that has never left me." Jack too has shared his thoughts and feelings, "As I reflect on the challenges and uncertainty that I and my teammates faced in that wondrous and unforgiving land, I am struck by its vastness and its beauty, and by the messages this quiet world daily spoke to me. I marvel also at how such a world gave rise to us in our prehistoric Ice Age past, and wonder endlessly about our—and God's—reality." The impact of this journey on all our lives is still evident in each of us.

On those occasions when we have been together, our remembrances inevitably touch on several topics, namely, our crevasse adventures on the Skelton Glacier, the loss of and injuries to our good Kiwi friends at the bottom of a crevasse, nature's beauty, the continent's insistent and pervasive power that threatened daily to end our expedition, and then the last day of our travel when Seismo and Mess Cat careened down monstrous rollers, narrowly and only by sheer luck, missing yawning huge crevasses. This last remembrance, we clearly understand, had all the makings of the disappearance of the Victoria Land Traverse. It could well have taken with it this story—and been the cause of our mysterious and final destiny.

Appendices

APPENDIX A. THE WILKES SUBGLACIAL BASIN

The Wilkes Subglacial Basin, discovered by the Victoria Land Traverse, 1959–1960, is a major subglacial topographic trough, 1,600 kilometers long and 400 kilometers wide, extending from near the South Pole to the Southern Ocean on George V Coast (Weihaupt, 1961).

APPENDIX B. THE WILKES LAND ANOMALY

The Wilkes Land Anomaly (upper figure) is an unusually large, absolute magnitude, negative free-air gravity anomaly discovered by the Victoria Land Traverse. Believed initially to represent a subglacial meteoroid impact crater, subsequent research has revealed that the anomaly is substantially larger (lower figure) than originally determined. This feature has recently been reclassified on the Impact Database as a probable impact crater on the basis of new research (Weihaupt et al., 2010; used with permission).

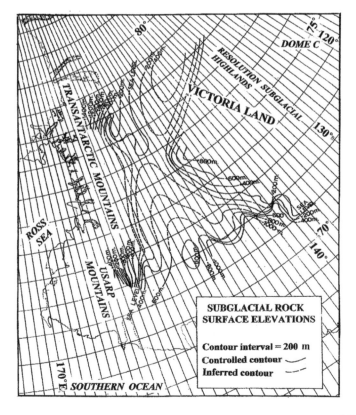

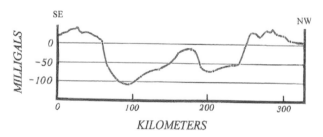

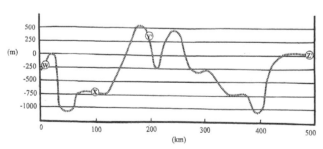

117

APPENDIX C. THE ORONTIUS FINAEUS MAP AND DISCOVERY OF ANTARCTICA

Research that originated from the Victoria Land Traverse led to the discovery of the Orontius Finaeus map of 1531, which meant that the discovery date of Antarctica was off by three centuries. Previously, it was believed that American and British whalers and sealers had discovered Antarctica in 1820. Therefore, the discovery of the Finaeus map discovery has revised the history of Antarctic exploration (Weihaupt and Pappamarinopoulos, 2008a; used with permission).

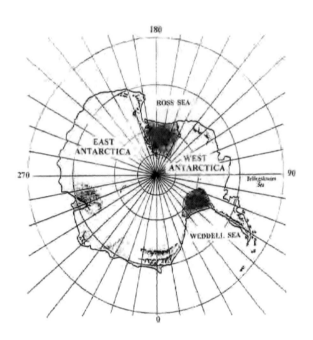

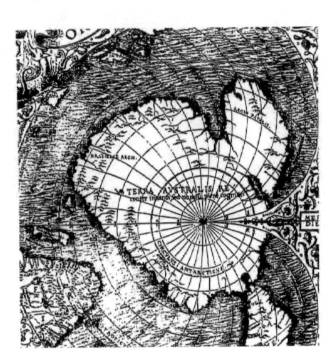

APPENDIX D. REGION OF CHAOTIC ICE: "THREADING THE NEEDLE"

The region of chaotic ice, where the VLT team encountered the "threading of the needle" terrain (see Fig. 8.7), reported by the U.S. Navy VX-6 Squadron crew. The members of the VLT team were unable to see the heavy crevassing from their vantage point along the traverse route. This photograph, from the National Aeronautics and Space Administration satellite imagery not available in 1960, does not reveal much of the heavy crevassing at this resolution because of the great elevation of the satellite. (Courtesy of the National Aeronautics and Space Administration.)

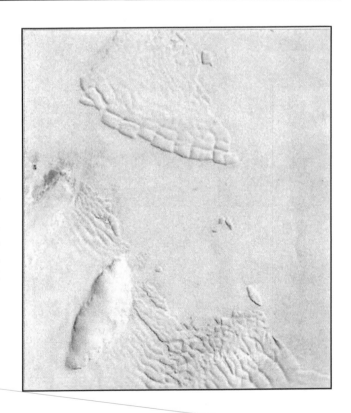

APPENDIX E. CRATERFORM SUBGLACIAL TOPOGRAPHY

The complex subglacial topography discovered in the region of the Wilkes Land Anomaly and the region of chaotic ice is evident in seismic, gravity, radiosound, and satellite remote-sensing data. Originally suggested to be a meteoroid impact structure, it has been reclassified from a "possible" to a "probable" impact structure (Rajmon, 2011, personal communication) on the basis of more recent research (Weihaupt et al., 2010; used with permission).

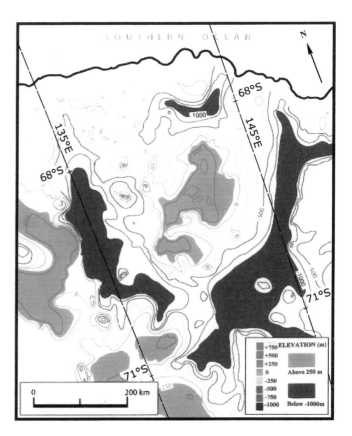

APPENDIX F. FREE-AIR GRAVITY CONTOUR MAP OF ANTARCTICA

Free-air gravity anomaly contour map of the Antarctic continent and offshore oceanic sectors (gravity anomaly values are in milligals). The negative free-air gravity anomalies range from approximately –10 mgal to –60 mgal, the greatest absolute negative values distributed in the Wilkes Land–Ross Sea sectors. The lower absolute negative free-air gravity anomaly values are distributed in the Weddell Sea sector, and the lowest absolute negative free-air gravity anomalies and the largely positive anomalies are distributed in the offshore circum-continental sector and range from –20 to +20 mgal. (Constructed from Challenging Minisatellite Payload System [CHAMPS] global positioning system [GPS], European Improved Gravity model of the Earth by New Techniques [EIGEN-1S] Satellite data, Projektbereich 1.3, Potsdam.) (After Weihaupt et al., 2010.)

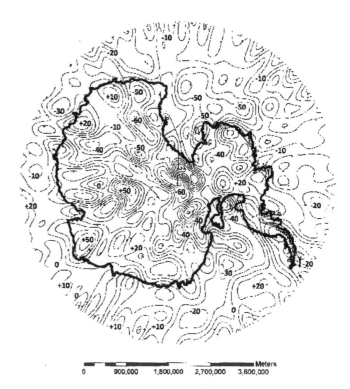

120 *Appendices*

APPENDIX G. FREE-AIR GRAVITY COLOR MAP OF ANTARCTICA

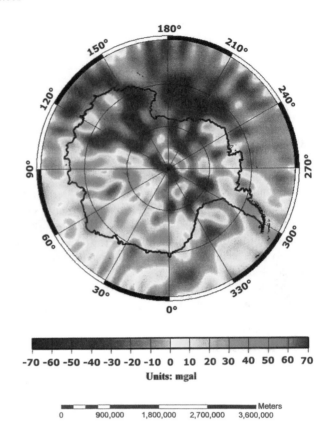

Antarctic free-air gravity anomaly map showing the pattern, distribution, and relative locations of negative free-air gravity anomalies (blue), and largely positive free-air gravity anomalies (yellow) mainly offshore and around the Antarctic continent. (From Weihaupt et al., 2010; used with permission.)

-70 -60 -50 -40 -30 -20 -10 0 10 20 30 40 50 60 70
Units: mgal

0   900,000   1,800,000   2,700,000   3,600,000   Meters

APPENDIX H. OUTBACK NUNATAKS

The Outback Nunataks, named by the Advisory Committee on Antarctic Names (US-ACAN) in 1961, were discovered by the Victoria Land Traverse late in the austral summer of 1960, and several of the mountains were named by the committee for members of the traverse team. (Courtesy of the U.S. Geological Survey.)

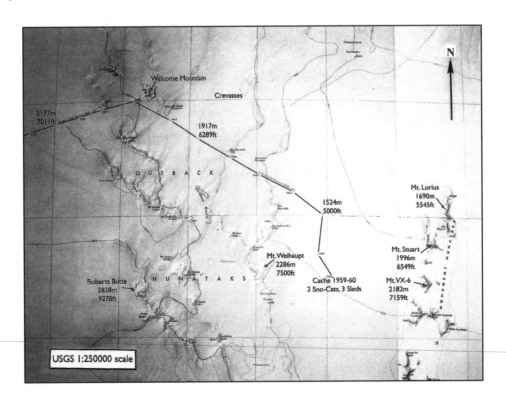

APPENDIX I. USARP MOUNTAINS

The USARP Mountains, named by the Advisory Committee on Antarctic Names (US-ACAN) in 1961, were discovered by the Victoria Land Traverse late in the austral summer of 1960 as the traverse approached the Transantarctic Mountains. (Courtesy of the U.S. National Aeronautics and Space Administration.)

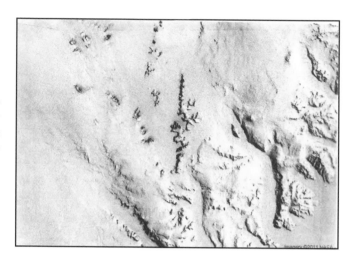

APPENDIX J. FINAL VICTORIA LAND TRAVERSE ROUTE

The final route of the Victoria Land Traverse from Scott Base via the Skelton Glacier to the Victoria Land Plateau and the Transantarctic Mountains. Each of the major stations is identified, and the contours represent ice surface elevations in meters.

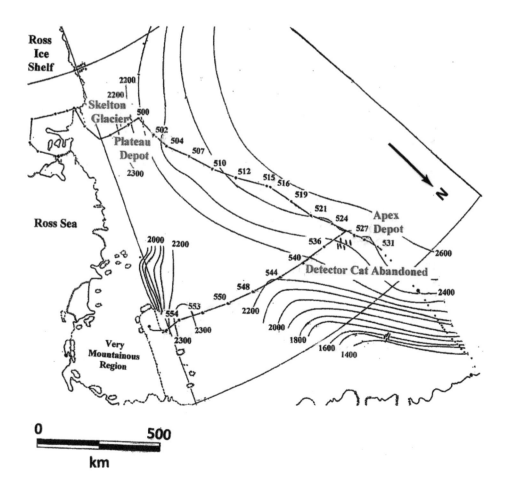

APPENDIX K. SEISMIC REFLECTION AND REFRACTION SOUNDINGS RECORDED AT MAJOR STATIONS
ON THE VICTORIA LAND TRAVERSE

Station	Latitude (in degrees and minutes)	Longitude (in degrees and minutes)	Ice surface elevation (meters)	Rock surface elevation (meters)	Ice thickness (meters)
502	77°27.8′	153°06′	2,371	315	2,056
504	77°02.1′	152°19′	2,437	−17	2,454
507	76°27.0′	150°24′	2,479	170	2,309
510	75°47.3′	148°27′	2,490	−50	2,540
512	75°12.1′	146°49′	2,520	702	1,818
515	74°34.1′	144°24′	2,590	697	1,893
519	(Not available)	(Not available)	2,541	575	1,966
521	72°57.1′	142°12′	2,509	262	2,254
524	72°28.7′	141°21′	2,498	348	2,150
527	71°50.2′	140°15′	2,467	−415	2,882
531 (B-61)	71°07.8′	139°11′	2,513	250	2,263
536	72°06.5′	143°12′	2,356	−898	3,254
540	72°08.0′	145°53′	2,287	−510	2,797
544	72°07.8′	148°12′	2,216	−580	2,796
546	72°09.0′	149°02′	2,170	−1130	3,300
550	72°14 2′	153°48′	2,220	−770	2,990
553	72°17.3′	156°22′	2,262	−215	2,477
554	72°19.0′	156°27′	2,309	−520	2,829
559	72°37.8′	161°32′	1,720	340	1,380

Notes: From these data, ice thicknesses were determined and identified by latitude, longitude, surface elevation, and subglacial rock surface elevation. Data provided by J. Weihaupt from personal field notes.

APPENDIX L. GLACIOLOGICAL SNOW ACCUMULATION DATA COLLECTED FROM PITS DUG
AT EACH MAJOR STATION ON THE VICTORIA LAND TRAVERSE

Station	Centimeters	Inches	Number of years	Notes
502	13.9	5.4	2	Inland from Skelton Glacier
504	16.2	6.4	1	
507	7.1	2.8	3	
510	13.2	5.2	7	
512	10.1	4.0	3	
515	20.5	8.1	6	
519	14.8	5.8	8	
521	11.7	4.6	9	
524	17.1	6.7	6	
527	14.8	5.8	9	
531 (B-61)	14.8	5.8	8	French flag–turnaround
536	17.8	7.0	6	
540	20.7	8.1	6	
544	16.3	6.4	7	Detector Cat abandoned
550	19.3	7.6	6	
553	17.8	7.0	7	
554	15.1	5.9	8	Welcome Mountain
559	16.3	6.4	5	Rennick Glacier
Average	15.6	6.2	6	

Notes: Accumulation estimates were determined from the snow pit and ice samples. Data provided by A. Stuart.

APPENDIX M. TRAVERSE STATION NUMBERS, LOCATIONS, AND ELEVATIONS

Station	Latitude (in degrees and minutes)	Longitude (in degrees and minutes)	Elevation (meters)
500	78°02.2′	154°06′	2,276
500A	78°00.0′	154°02′	2,285
500B	77°56.8′	153°56′	2,290
500C	77°54.1′	153°52′	2,294
500D	77°52.1′	153°47′	2,305
500E	77°50.0′	153°44′	2,311
500F	77°47.5′	153°40′	2,337
500G	77°45.3′	153°36′	2,339
501	77°41.5′	153°29′	2,336
501A	77°40.0′	153°26′	2,342
501B	77°37.3′	153°22′	2,343
501C	77°34.8′	153°18′	2,344
501D	77°32.1′	153°13′	2,362
501E	77°29.2′	153°08′	2,366
502	77°27.8′	153°06′	2,371
502A	77°25.0′	153°01′	2,383
502B	77°22.5′	152°56′	2,397
502C	77°20.0′	152°52′	2,401
502D	77°17.5′	152°47′	2,411
502E	77°14.8′	152°42′	2,425
502F	77°12.0′	152°37′	2,429
503	77°09.0′	152°33′	2,435
503A	77°06.8′	152°27′	2,435
504	77°02.1′	152°19′	2,437
504A	77°00.5′	152°14′	2,440
504B	76°58.2′	152°06′	2,452
504C	76°56.0′	151°59′	2,459
504D	76°53.7′	151°51′	2,460
505	76°52.0′	151°46′	2,463
505A	76°50.3′	151°41′	2,464
505B	76°48.5′	151°35′	2,467
505C	76°47.0′	151°30′	2,466
505D	76°46.1′	151°27′	2,467
505E	76°44.2′	151°21′	2,468
505F	76°42.2′	151°15′	2,469
505G	76°40.5′	151°10′	2,473
505H	76°38.5′	151°03′	2,472
505I	76°36.2′	150°55′	2,474
506	76°35.3′	150°53′	2,476
506A	76°32.7′	150°43′	2,479
506B	76°30.1′	150°34′	2,482
507	76°27.0′	150°24′	2,479
507A	76°25.0′	150°18′	2,481
507B	76°22.7′	150°10′	2,480
507C	76°20.5′	150°04′	2,479
507D	76°19.0′	149°58′	2,477
507E	76°16.7′	149°51′	2,477
508	76°15.5′	149°47′	2,474
508A	76°13.5′	149°42′	2,479
508B	76°11.3′	149°35′	2,470
508C	76°09.7′	149°30′	2,471
509	76°07.5′	149°23′	2,468
509A	76°05.0′	149°16′	2,467
509B	76°02.7′	149°09′	2,470
509C	76°00.0′	149°02′	2,469
509D	75°57.2′	148°54′	2,467
509E	75°54.8′	148°46′	2,469
509F	75°51.0′	148°38′	2,482
510	75°47.3′	148°27′	2,490
510A	75°45.4′	148°19′	2,487
510B	75°43.3′	148°12′	2,487
510C	75°46.1′	148°04′	2,491
510D	75°38.9′	147°56′	2,499
510E	75°36.7′	147°48′	2,508
510F	75°34.2′	147°40′	2,508
510G	75°32.0′	147°32′	2,512
511	75°30.5′	147°26′	2,517
511A	75°27.0′	147°18′	2,512
511B	75°24.5′	147°14′	2,509
511C	75°21.1′	147°07′	2,510
511D	75°18.0′	147°00′	2,515
511E	75°14.5′	146°52′	2,523
512	75°12.1′	146°49′	2,520
512A	75°10.5′	146°44′	2,511

(Continued)

APPENDIX M. TRAVERSE STATION NUMBERS, LOCATIONS, AND
ELEVATIONS (*Continued*)

Station	Latitude (in degrees and minutes)	Longitude (in degrees and minutes)	Elevation (meters)
512B	75°07.8′	146°34′	2,517
512C	75°04.5′	146°25′	2,517
512D	75°01.8′	146°16′	2,524
512E	74°58.5′	146°08′	2,535
512F	74°55.6′	145°59′	2,539
513	74°53.0′	145°52′	2,549
513A	74°50.8′	145°44′	2,559
513B	74°48.2′	145°35′	2,552
513C	74°41.3′	145°28′	2,554
513D	74°44.2′	145°20′	2,568
513E	74°41.8′	145°12′	2,572
513F	74°39.5′	145°05′	2,573
513G	74°37.3′	144°57′	2,577
514	74°36.0′	144°52′	2,581
514A	74°34.5′	144°46′	2,586
514B	74°32.3′	144°43′	2,590
514C	74°34.1′	144°26′	2,590
515	74°34.1′	144°24′	2,590
521D	72°57.1′	142°12′	2,509
521E	72°54.5′	142°07′	2,506
521F	72°51.6′	142°02′	2,503
521G	72°49.3′	141°58′	2,500
522	72°46.3′	141°54′	2,506
522A	72°45.7′	141°53′	2,504
522B	72°43.4′	141°48′	2,499
522C	72°41.6′	141°45′	2,496
522D	72°40.0′	141°42′	2,497
522E	72°38.9′	141°40′	2,497
523	72°38.0′	141°38′	2,498
523A	72°36.4′	141°35′	2,503
523B	72°35.2′	141°32′	2,504
523C	72°33.8′	141°29′	2,502
523D	72°32.0′	141°25′	2,596
523E	72°30.7′	141°22′	2,494
523F	72°29.0′	141°20′	2,495
524	72°28.7′	141°21′	2,498
524A	72°26.1′	141°15′	2,502
524B	72°23.8′	141°10′	2,502
524C	72°21.0′	141°06′	2,488
524D	72°18.5′	141°02′	2,493
525	72°15.8′	140°56′	2,491
525A	72°13.2′	140°52′	2,500
525B	72°11.0′	140°48′	2,510
525C	72°08.1′	140°44′	2,515
525D	72°05.8′	140°39′	2,501
525E	72°03.2′	140°35′	2,514
525F	72°00.3′	140°30′	2,494
526	71°58.0′	140°27′	2,482
526A	71°55.2′	140°23′	2,472
526B	71°53.0′	140°20′	2,470
527	71°50.2′	140°15′	2,467
527A	71°47.6′	140°12′	2,469
527B	71°45.0′	140°10′	2,465
528	71°42.2′	140°06′	2,467
528A	71°39.3′	140°04′	2,471
528B	71°37.1′	140°01′	2,466
528C	71°34.5′	139°57′	2,465
528D	71°31.9′	139°54′	2,469
529	71°29.6′	139°54′	2,458
529A	71°27.0′	139°50′	2,453
529B	71°24.2′	139°46′	2,459
529C	71°21.8′	139°41′	2,461
529D	71°19.3′	139°37′	2,474
529E	71°16.7′	139°32′	2,478
530	71°14.0′	139°28′	2,487
530A	71°11.6′	139°22′	2,498
530B	71°10.0′	139°18′	2,509
530C	71°09.2′	139°16′	2,511
531 (B-61)	71°07.8′	139°11′	2,513

[Track re-traced from Station 531 back to Station 525F; same data as above] (*Continued*)

APPENDIX M. TRAVERSE STATION NUMBERS, LOCATIONS, AND
ELEVATIONS (*Continued*)

Station	Latitude (in degrees and minutes)	Longitude (in degrees and minutes)	Elevation (meters)
532	72°01.8′	140°34′	2,507
532A	72°01.8′	140°40′	2,494
532B	72°01.8′	140°47′	2,476
532C	72°01.8′	140°53′	2,465
532D	72°01.8′	141°00′	2,468
532E	72°01.8′	141°06′	2,481
533	72°01.8′	141°08′	2,477
533A	72°01.8′	141°14′	2,469
533B	72°01.9′	141°20′	2,463
533C	72°02.2′	141°26′	2,449
533D	72°02.1′	141°32′	2,430
533E	72°02.2′	141°38′	2,424
533F	72°02.3′	141°44′	2,424
534	72°02.4′	141°45′	2,422
534A	72°02.4′	141°52′	2,418
534B	72°02.5′	141°58′	2,415
534C	72°02.6′	142°04′	2,404
534D	72°02.7′	142°10′	2,390
534E	72°02.8′	142°16′	2,386
534F	72°02.9′	142°23′	2,384
534G	72°03.0′	142°29′	2,383
535	72°03.0′	142°33′	2,383
535A	72°03.5′	142°39′	2,378
535B	72°04.0′	142°45′	2,373
535C	72°04.5′	142°50′	2,370
535D	72°05.0′	142°56′	2,364
535E	72°05.5′	143°02′	2,362
535F	72°06.0′	143°08′	2,359
536	72°06.5′	143°12′	2,356
536A	72°06.4′	143°18′	2,352
536B	72°06.3′	143°24′	2,349
536C	72°06.2′	143°32′	2,346
536D	72°06.1′	143°38′	2,346
536E	72°06.1′	143°42′	2,346
537	72°06.0′	143°51′	2,351
537A	72°06.2′	143°58′	2,344
537B	72°06.4′	144°04′	2,328
537C	72°06.6′	144°11′	2,329
537D	72°06.8′	144°17′	2,329
538	72°07.0′	144°23′	2,328
538A	72°07.0′	144°30′	2,325
538B	72°07.0′	144°36′	2,327
538C	72°07.1′	144°42′	2,324
538D	72°07.1′	144°49′	2,328
538E	72°07.1′	144°55′	2,324
538F	72°07.2′	145°02′	2,314
538G	72°07.2′	145°08′	2,309
538H	72°07.2′	145°14′	2,313
539	72°07.2′	145°20′	2,309
539A	72°07.4′	145°27′	2,309
539B	72°07.6′	145°33′	2,304
539C	72°07.7′	145°38′	2,298
539D	72°07.8′	145°43′	2,291
539E	72°07.9′	145°48′	2,291
540	72°08.0′	145°53′	2,287
540A	72°08.1′	146°00′	2,280
541	72°08.2′	146°05′	2,273
541A	72°08.2′	146°11′	2,268
541B	72°08.2′	146°17′	2,263
541C	72°08.2′	146°23′	2,266
541D	72°08.1′	146°30′	2,262
541E	72°08.1′	146°33′	2,261
541F	72°08.1′	146°40′	2,258
541G	72°08.0′	146°47′	2,251
541H	72°08.0′	146°52′	2,246
541I	72°08.0′	146°59′	2,232
542	72°08.0′	147°05′	2,225
542A	72°07.8′	147°12′	2,227
542B	72°07.6′	147°18′	2,224
542C	72°07.4′	147°24′	2,227
542D	72°07.2′	147°31′	2,226
543	72°07.0′	147°36′	2,222
543A	72°07.1′	147°44′	2,219
543B	72°07.3′	147°50′	2,223

(*Continued*)

APPENDIX M. TRAVERSE STATION NUMBERS, LOCATIONS, AND
ELEVATIONS (*Continued*)

Station	Latitude (in degrees and minutes)	Longitude (in degrees and minutes)	Elevation (meters)
543C	72°07.4′	147°56′	2,226
543D	72°07.6′	148°03′	2,223
543E	72°07.7′	148°08′	2,217
544	72°07.8′	148°12′	2,216
544A	72°07.8′	148°20′	2,211
544B	72°07.9′	148°26′	2,208
544C	72°07.9′	148°31′	2,206
545	72°08.0′	148°34′	2,199
545A	72°08.2′	148°40′	2,191
545B	72°08.4′	148°47′	2,173
545C	72°08.6′	148°52′	2,163
545D	72°08.8′	148°58′	2,170
546	72°09.0′	149°02′	2,170
546A	72°09.2′	149°09′	2,170
546B	72°09.4′	149°15′	2,170
546C	72°09.6′	149°21′	2,180
546D	72°09.8′	149°26′	2,194
546E	72°10.0′	149°33′	2,201
546F	72°10.2′	149°40′	2,207
546G	72°10.4′	149°48′	2,206
546H	72°10.7′	149°56′	2,207
547	72°11.0′	150°06′	2,206
547A	72°11.1′	150°19′	2,204
547B	72°11.3′	150°32′	2,211
547C	72°11.5′	150°46′	2,209
547D	72°11.7′	151°01′	2,207
548	72°11.8′	151°14′	2,205
548A	72°12.0′	151°27′	2,203
548B	72°12.2′	151°38′	2,208
548C	72°12.4′	151°50′	2,210
548D	72°12.6′	152°03′	2,214
548E	72°12.8′	152°14′	2,217
549	72°13.0′	152°28′	2,223
549A	72°13.1′	152°40′	2,222
549B	72°13.3′	152°51′	2,223
549C	72°13.4′	152°57′	2,229
549D	72°13.6′	153°08′	2,229
549E	72°13.7′	153°19′	2,231
549F	72°13.9′	153°30′	2,225
549G	72°14.0′	153°38′	2,224
550	72°14.2′	153°48′	2,220
550A	72°14.4′	154°01′	2,224
550B	72°14.6′	154°12′	2,223
550C	72°14.8′	154°21′	2,217
551	72°15.0′	154°30′	2,231
551A	72°15.5′	154°43′	2,239
551B	72°15.7′	154°48′	2,237
552	72°16.0′	154°53′	2,237
552A	72°16.1′	155°00′	2,238
552B	72°16.3′	155°10′	2,243
552C	72°16.4′	155°19′	2,247
552D	71°16.5′	155°30′	2,252
552E	72°16.7′	155°40′	2,248
552F	72°16.9′	155°54′	2,261
552G	72°17.1′	156°06′	2,258
553	72°17.3′	156°22′	2,262
553A	72°17.6′	156°32′	2,269
553B	72°17.9′	156°45′	2,272
553C	72°18.1′	156°54′	2,280
553D	72°18.4′	156°06′	2,279
553E	72°18.7′	156°16′	2,298
554	72°19.0′	156°27′	2,309
554A	72°19.2′	156°37′	2,304
554B	72°19.4′	156°46′	2,303
554C	72°19.5′	156°51′	2,315
554D	72°19.7′	158°06′	2,323
555	72°20.0′	158°12′	2,328
555A	72°21.0′	158°24′	2,331
555B	72°21.9′	158°35′	2,333
556	72°22.6′	156°45′	2,331
556A	72°21.0′	159°00′	2,327
556B	72°19.5′	159°15′	2,319
556C	72°19.0′	159°18′	2,304

(*Continued*)

APPENDIX M. TRAVERSE STATION NUMBERS, LOCATIONS, AND
ELEVATIONS (*Continued*)

Station	Latitude (in degrees and minutes)	Longitude (in degrees and minutes)	Elevation (meters)
556D	72°18.1'	159°29'	2,265
556E	72°17.2'	159°40'	2,235
557	72°16.3'	159°49'	2,213
557A	72°15.5'	160°04'	2,194
558	72°15.1'	160°08'	2,198
558A	72°17.8'	160°24'	2,072
558B	72°20.2'	160°36'	2,045
558C	72°22.8'	160°50'	1,917
558D	72°25.0'	161°02'	1,761
558E	72°27.2'	161°16'	1,681
558F	72°30.0'	161°28'	1,652
558G	72°35.0'	161°26'	1,696
559	72°37.8'	161°32'	1,720

Note: Station locations and elevations were recorded at all major stations and at all intermediate traverse stops. These data were provided by J. Weihaupt from field data, and later data reductions.

APPENDIX N. PUBLICATIONS RESULTING FROM THE VICTORIA LAND TRAVERSE

Lorius, C., 1983, Antarctica; survey of near surface mean isotopic values, *in* Robin, G. de Q., ed., The Climatic Record in Polar Ice Sheets: A Study of Isotopic and Temperature Profiles in Polar Ice Sheets Based on a Workshop Held in the Scott Polar Research Institute, Cambridge: Cambridge, UK, Cambridge University Press, p. 1–13.

Lorius, C., 1984, Data from Antarctic ice core on CO_2, climate aerosols and changes in ice thickness: Annals of Glaciology, v. 5, p. 49–62.

Lorius, C., 1991, Glaces de l'Antarctique: Une Mémoire, des Passions: Paris, O. Jacob, 301 p. (in French).

Lorius, C., and Gendrin, R., 1997, L'Antarctique: Flammarion, 127 p. (in French).

Lorius, C., Merlivat, L., Jouzel, J., and Pourchet, M., 1979, A 30,000 yr isotope climatic record from Antarctic ice: Nature, v. 280, p. 644–648, doi:10.1038/280644a0.

Lorius, C., Barkov, N.I., Jouzel, J., Korotkevich, Y.S., Kotlyakov, V.M., and Raynaud, D., 1988, Antarctic ice core: CO_2 and climatic change over the last climatic cycle: Eos (Transactions, American Geophysical Union), v. 69, no. 26, p. 681–684, doi:10.1029/88EO00230.

Lorius, C., Jouzel, J., Raynaud, D., Hansen, J., and Le Treut, H., 1990, The ice-core record: Climate sensitivity and future greenhouse warming: Nature, v. 347, p. 139–145, doi:10.1038/347139a0.

Lorius, C., Jouzel, J., and Raynaud, D., 1992, The ice core record: Past archive of the climate and signpost to the future: Philosophical Transactions of the Royal Society of London, ser. B, v. 338, p. 227–234, doi:10.1098/rstb.1992.0142.

Petit, J.R., Duval, P., and Lorius, C., 1987, Long-term climatic changes indicated by crystal growth in polar ice: Nature, v. 326, p. 62–64, doi:10.1038/326062a0.

Raynaud, D., Jouzel, J., Barnola, J.-M., Chappellaz, J., Delmas, R.J., and Lorius, C., 1993, The ice record of greenhouse gases: Science, v. 259, p. 926–934.

Smith, W.M., 1966, Observations over the lifetime of a small isolated group: Structure, danger, boredom, and vision: Psychological Reports, Monograph Supplement 3-V19, p. 6–12.

Stuart, A.W., 2007, This Frozen World: The Polar Diaries of Alfred Wright Stuart: Pipes & Timbrels Press, 133 p.

Stuart, A.W., and Bull, C., 1963, Glaciological observations on the Ross Ice Shelf near Scott Base, Antarctica: Journal of Glaciology, v. 4, no. 34, p. 399–414.

Stuart, A.W., and Heine, A.J., 1961a, Glaciological work of the 1959–1960 U.S.: Victoria Land Traverse: Journal of Glaciology, v. 3, no. 30, p. 997–1002.

Stuart, A.W., and Heine, A.J., 1961b, Glaciology, Victoria Land Traverse, 1959–1960: Ohio State University Research Foundation Report, v. 968, Part I, p. 1–52.

Weihaupt, J.G., 1960a, Victoria Land Traverse Logistics: Arctic Institute of North America, Technical Report to the National Science Foundation, p. 1–13.

Weihaupt, J.G., 1960b, Victoria Land Traverse, Antarctica, 1959–60: Arctic, v. 13, no. 2, p. 1–20.

Weihaupt, J.G., 1960c, Reconnaissance of a newly discovered area of mountains in Antarctica: The Journal of Geology, v. 68, no. 6, p. 669–673, doi:10.1086/626704.

Weihaupt, J.G., 1961a, Geophysical Studies in Victoria Land, Antarctica: Geophysical and Polar Research Center, Madison, University of Wisconsin, Research Report No. 1, p. 1–123.

Weihaupt, J.G., 1961b, Two recently discovered glaciers, Antarctica: Arctic, v. 14, no. 2, p. 120–123.

Weihaupt, J.G., 1963, Seismic and gravity studies at the South Pole: Geophysics, v. 28, no. 4, p. 582–592, doi:10.1190/1.1439232.

Weihaupt, J.G., 1976a, Evidence for a giant Antarctic meteorite in Recent geologic time, *in* Transactions of the 25th International Geological Congress, Sydney, Australia, v. 25, p. 1–12.

Weihaupt, J.G., 1976b, The Wilkes Land Anomaly: Evidence for a possible hypervelocity impact crater: Journal of Geophysical Research, v. 81, no. 32, p. 5651–5663, doi:10.1029/JB081i032p05651.

Weihaupt, J.G., 1978, Elgytgyn crater, Siberia: Probable source of Australian tektites, Comment on: Meteoritics, v. 13, no. 1, p. 163.

Weihaupt, J.G., 1984, Historic cartographic evidence for Holocene changes in the Antarctic ice cover: Eos (Transactions, American Geophysical Union), v. 65, no. 35, p. 493–501, doi:10.1029/EO065i035p00493.

Weihaupt, J.G., 1985a, Apollo impact events as causes of biospheric catastrophe, *in* Baity, E.C., ed., Ancient Civilizations and Extreme Natural Events: Austin, University of Texas Press.

Weihaupt, J.G., 1985b, Of maps and men: Antarctic clues from our medieval past: Research Newsletter, Society of Sigma Xi, v. 2, no. 1.

Weihaupt, J.G., 1985c, The Wilkes Land Anomaly: Evidence for a possible hypervelocity impact crater, *in* Baity, E.C., ed., Ancient Civilizations and Extreme Natural Events: Austin, University of Texas Press. (Reprint of Weihaupt, 1976b.)

Weihaupt, J.G., 1998, Ice sheet disintegration evidence for higher world-wide sea level stand prior to A.D. 1500, *in* Monsó de Prat, J.L., ed., Littoral '98, Proceedings of EUROCOAST/ASINCA, September 14–17, 1998, Barcelona, Spain, p. 269–274.

Weihaupt, J.G., and Chambers, F.B., 2001, Cause of rapid East Antarctic glacier tongue responses: Earth System Processes, Proceedings of the Geological Society of America and the Geological Society of London, June 24–28, 2001, Edinburgh, Scotland, Earth System Processes Conference, p. 59.

Weihaupt, J.G., and Papamarinopoulos, S., 2008a, The strange and undocumented discoveries of Antarctica and South America: Part I, a historic-enigma, *in* Papamarinopoulos, S., ed., The Atlantis Hypothesis, 2nd International Conference, November 10–11, 2008, Athens, Greece: Heliotopos Publications, p. 727–738.

Weihaupt, J.G., and Papamarinopoulos, S., 2008b, The strange and undocumented discoveries of Antarctica and South America: Part II, the evidence, *in* Papamarinopoulos, S., ed., The Atlantis Hypothesis, 2nd International Conference, November 10–11, 2008, Athens, Greece, Heliotopos Publications, p. 739–746.

Weihaupt, J.G., and Rice, A., 2000a, Antarctic coastline variability: Dramatic regional decline, *in* Lee, S.S., ed., Living with Diversity, Proceedings of the 29th International Geological Congress, August 14–18, Seoul, Korea, p. 52.

Weihaupt, J.G., and Rice, A., 2000b, Antarctic glacier tongue recession, *in* Cordani, U.G., ed., Geology and Sustainable Development: Challenges for the Third Millennium, Proceedings of the 31st International Geological Congress, August 6–17, 2000, Rio de Janeiro, Brazil, p. 200.

Weihaupt, J.G., and Rice, A., 2007, Suggestions of multiple meteoroid impact in Antarctica: How do we sort it out? *in* Proceedings of the 31st Symposium on Antarctic Meteorites, June 5–7, 2007, National Institute of Polar Research, Tokyo, Japan, p. 37.

Weihaupt, J.G., and Stuart, A.W., 2000, Future global coastline changes implied in historic archives, *in* Požar-Domac, A., ed., Responsible Coastal Zone Management—The Challenge of the 21ˢᵗ Century: Periodicum Biologogorum, Zagreb, v. 102, p. 439–448.

Weihaupt, J.G., and Stuart, A.W., 2001, Uncertainty in the historic time scale of global warming and sea level rise, *in* Eleventh Conference of the International Society for the Study of Time, Costello de Gargonza, Italy.

Weihaupt, J.G., and Stuart, A.W., 2002, Century scale variations in the Mertz and Ninnis Glacier Tongues, Antarctica: Global sea level implications, *in* Gomes, F.B., ed., Littoral 2002, The Changing Coast: Porto, Portugal, European Coastal Association for Science and Technology (EUROCOAST/EUCC) September 22–26, 2002, p. 141–147.

Weihaupt, J.G., and Van der Hoeven, F.G., 2004a, Catastrophic disruption of the Antarctic continental ice sheet and potential global sea level rise, *in* Delivering Sustainable Coasts: Connecting Science and Policy, Proceedings of the Littoral Conference of the European Coastal Union (EUCC) and the European Coastal Zone Association for Science and Technology (EUROCOAST): Aberdeen, Scotland, p. 106.

Weihaupt, J.G., and Van der Hoeven, F.G., 2004b, Global sea level variation as a function of catastrophic perturbation of the Antarctic continental ice sheet, *in* 30th International Geographical Union, University of Glasgow, Scotland.

Weihaupt, J.G., and Van der Hoeven, F.G., 2004c, The Antarctic gravity spectrum: Mantle, lithosphere, and crustal considerations, *in* Abbati, E., ed., From the Mediterranean Area toward a Global Geological Renaissance: Geology, Natural Hazards, and Cultural Heritage, Proceedings of the 32nd International Geological Congress, August 20–28, 2004, Forteza da Basso, Florence, Italy, p. 159.

Weihaupt, J.G., Rice, A., and Van der Hoeven, F.G., 2006, Multiple meteoroid impact in Antarctica? *in* Proceedings of the American Geophysical Union Meeting, December 2006, San Francisco.

Weihaupt, J.G., Rice, A., and Van der Hoeven, F.G., 2009, Multiple meteoroid impacts in Antarctica: Potential for major glacial surges? *in* Natural Hazards, Proceedings of the American Geophysical Union Meeting, December 11–19, 2009, San Francisco, p. 71.

Weihaupt, J.G., Rice, A., and Van der Hoeven, F.G., 2010a, Gravity anomalies of the Antarctic lithosphere: Lithosphere, v. 2, no. 6, p. 454–461, doi:10.1130/L116.1.

Weihaupt, J.G., Rice, A., and Van der Hoeven, F.G., 2010b, Multiple meteoroid impacts in Antarctica and the mid-Brunhes Event/mis 11 Stage: If there's a connection, what are the implications for humanity? The Meeting of the Americas, Proceedings, August 8–13, 2010, Foz do Iguassu, Brazil, p. 76.

Weihaupt, J.G., Rice, A., and Van der Hoeven, F.G., 2010c, Multiple meteoroid impacts in Antarctica at 481,000ky: A possible cause for the mid-Brunhes Event/MIS 11 Stage via the disruption of the West Anatarctic Ice Sheet? [abs.], *in* Proceedings of the Annual Meeting of the American Geophysical Union, December 13–7, 2010, San Francisco, p. 474.

Weihaupt, J.G., Rice, A., and Van der Hoeven, F., 2010d, Were bolide impacts in Antarctica responsible for the apparent loss of the WAIS at the Mid-Brunhes Event/MIS 11 stage?: Geological Society of America Abstracts with Programs, v. 42, no. 5, p. 32

Glossary

Ablation   Removal of snow or ice by melting, evaporation, or sublimation.

Anomaly   Departure from that which is standard or normal.

Aurora Australis   Aurora that occurs in the southern regions of Earth; also called southern lights.

Crevasse   Deep crevice or fissure in a glacier or continental ice sheet.

Crevasse detector   Device designed to detect crevasses, particularly when crevasses are concealed by an overlying snow bridge.

Geomagnetic field   Earth's magnetic field, which is an approximate dipole with one end at the South Magnetic Pole and the other at the North Magnetic Pole.

Geophone   An electronic receiver designed to detect seismic vibrations.

Gravimeter   An instrument designed to measure gravitational acceleration and to detect changes in gravitational acceleration from one place to another.

Impact Database   Comprehensive list of proposed and confirmed meteorite impact sites on Earth.

International Geophysical Year (IGY)   An international scientific program involving numerous nations from July 1, 1957, to December 31, 1958.

Ionosphere   A layer in Earth's atmosphere containing high concentrations of ions and free electrons capable of reflecting radio waves emitted from Earth's surface.

Isotope analysis   Determination of species and amounts of isotopes in materials and objects.

Katabatic wind   A cold, downslope wind, often generated by an atmospheric high-pressure system like that which remains over the center of the Antarctic continent.

Morse code   An alphabetic code in which letters are represented by combinations of long and short signals of sound or light.

Nitramon   An explosive mixture based upon ammonium nitrate used for the generation of seismic energy for the purpose of creating signals from a reflective surface, such as subsurface

layers in sedimentary rocks or rock surfaces beneath a continental ice sheet.

Radar reflector   A device that reflects electromagnetic signals, in particular radar signals.

Ramsonde   Cone-tipped metal rod driven into snow to determine its hardness and density; also called a ram penetrometer.

Reflection shot   A geophysical exploration technique involving the detonation of an explosive or otherwise generated impulse that will return a reflected signal.

Refraction shot   A geophysical exploration technique involving the detonation of an explosive to generate an impulse that will be refracted by subsurface sedimentary or other horizontal layers such as ice stratigraphic units in a continental ice sheet.

Rolligon   Rolling fuel transporter consisting of large tires capable of containing fuel.

Sastrugi   Parallel, wavelike ridges and other promontories caused by winds on hard snow surfaces, especially in polar regions.

Seismogel   Water-gel explosive mixture composed of ammonium nitrate and methylammonium nitrate used for seismic exploration, in particular refraction seismic exploration.

Seismograph   An instrument designed to measure and record the force and duration of seismic waves.

Skua gull   Predatory sea birds of the genus *Catharacta*, commonly found in the coastal regions of Antarctica.

Snow bridge   Mass of snow that bridges a crevasse, usually caused by snow blowing over an open crevasse; often indistinguishable from the surrounding snow surface, therefore presenting a lurking danger for vehicles, persons, or animals traveling in the vicinity.

VX-6   U.S. Navy squadron in Antarctica with the mission of supporting scientific field investigations in the continental interior.

Windscoop   Moat-like depression in a snow surface at the base and surrounding a mountain, created by eroding winds.

References Cited

Lorius, C., 1991, Glaces de l'Antarctique: Une Mémoire, des Passions: Paris, O. Jacob, 301 p. (in French).

Lorius, C., and Gendrin, R., 1997, L'Antarctique: Flammarion, 127 p. (in French).

Lorius, C., Merlivat, L., Jouzel, J., and Pourchet, M., 1979, A 30,000 yr isotope climatic record from Antarctic ice: Nature, v. 280, p. 644–648, doi:10.1038/280644a0.

Lorius, C., Jouzel, J., Ritz, C., Merivat, L., Barkov, N.I., Korotkevich, Y.N., and Kotlyakof, V.M., 1985, A 150,000-year climatic record from Antarctic ice: Nature, v. 316, p. 591–596, doi:10.1038/316591a0.

Lorius, C., Jouzel, J., Raynaud, D., Hansen, J., and Le Treut, H., 1990, The ice-core record: Climate sensitivity and future greenhouse warming: Nature, v. 347, p. 139–145, doi:10.1038/347139a0.

Petit, J.R., Duval, P., and Lorius, C., 1987, Long-term climatic changes indicated by crystal growth in polar ice: Nature, v. 326, p. 62–64, doi:10.1038/326062a0.

Raynaud, D., Jouzel, J., Barnola, J.-M., Chappellaz, J., Delmas, R.J., and Lorius, C., 1993, The ice record of greenhouse gases: Science, v. 259, p. 926–934.

Weihaupt, J.G., 1961, Geophysical Studies in Victoria Land, Antarctica: Research Report No. 1, Geophysical and Polar Research Center, University of Wisconsin, 123 p.

Weihaupt, J.G., 1963, Seismic and gravity studies at the South Pole: Geophysics, v. 28, no. 4, p. 582–592, doi:10.1190/1.1439232.

Weihaupt, J.G., 1979, Exploration of the Oceans: An Introduction to Oceanography: New York, Macmillan Company, 589 p.

Weihaupt, J.G., 1984, Historic cartographic evidence for Holocene changes in the Antarctic ice cover: Eos (Transactions, American Geophysical Union), v. 65, no. 35, p. 493–501, doi:10.1029/EO065i035p00493.

Weihaupt, J.G., and Papamarinopoulos, S., 2008a, The strange and undocumented discoveries of Antarctica and South America: Part I: An historic enigma, in Papamarinopoulos, S., ed., The Atlantis Hypothesis, 2nd International Conference, November 10–11, 2008, Athens, Greece, Heliotopos Publications, p.727–738.

Weihaupt, J.G., and Papamarinopoulos, S., 2008b, The strange and undocumented discoveries of Antarctica and south America: Part II: The evidence, in Papamarinopoulos, S., ed., The Atlantis Hypothesis, 2nd International Conference, November 10–11, 2008, Athens, Greece, Heliotopos Publications, p. 739–746.

Weihaupt, J.G., Rice, A., and Van der Hoeven, F.G., 2010, Gravity anomalies of the Antarctic lithosphere: Lithosphere, v. 2, no. 6, p. 454–461, doi:10.1130/L116.1.

MANUSCRIPT ACCEPTED BY THE SOCIETY 3 JANUARY 2012

Index